SHADOW NATIONS

SHADOW NATIONS

Tribal Sovereignty and the Limits of Legal Pluralism

N. Bruce Duthu

OXFORD
UNIVERSITY PRESS

OXFORD
UNIVERSITY PRESS

Oxford University Press is a department of the University of Oxford.
It furthers the University's objective of excellence in research, scholarship,
and education by publishing worldwide.

Oxford New York
Auckland Cape Town Dar es Salaam Hong Kong Karachi
Kuala Lumpur Madrid Melbourne Mexico City Nairobi
New Delhi Shanghai Taipei Toronto

With offices in
Argentina Austria Brazil Chile Czech Republic France Greece
Guatemala Hungary Italy Japan Poland Portugal Singapore
South Korea Switzerland Thailand Turkey Ukraine Vietnam

Published in the United States of America by
Oxford University Press
198 Madison Avenue, New York, NY 10016

Library of Congress Cataloging-in-Publication Data

Duthu, N. Bruce.
Shadow nations : tribal sovereignty and the limits of legal pluralism / N. Bruce Duthu.
p. cm.
Includes bibliographical references.
ISBN 978–0–19–973586–0 (hardback : alk. paper)
1. Indians of North America—Legal status, laws, etc. 2. Indians of North America—Government relations. 3. Legal polycentricity—United States. 4. Sovereignty.
I. Title.
KF8205.D88 2013
342.7308′72—dc23
2012048896

9 8 7 6 5 4 3 2 1
Printed in the United States of America
on acid-free paper

For
Hilde, Lisa, Joe, and Alanna
and
Jim and Susan Wright

An optimist thinks that this is the best of all possible worlds. A pessimist fears that this is so.[1]

Contents

Acknowledgments

I am indebted to a number of scholars, colleagues, friends, and family who have contributed ideas, suggestions, and other forms of support throughout the research and writing of this book. First and foremost, I express my gratitude to Colin Calloway, my friend and colleague in Native American Studies at Dartmouth College, who introduced me to the editorial team at Oxford University Press. As a colleague and scholarly role model, Colin has no peer. David McBride and Sarah Rosenthal at Oxford were unfailingly generous and supportive of me throughout the entire writing and editing process. I would be hard-pressed to imagine working on this project with a better team of editors. My colleagues at Dartmouth College provided invaluable advice and direction on a number of research subjects. I extend thanks to Dale Turner and Vera Palmer in Native American Studies, Lucas Swaine and Sonu Bedi in Government, and Amy Allen in Philosophy.

Colleagues in other parts of the world generously shared resources and references that added immeasurably to my understanding of legal pluralism. In this regard, Rick Mohr in Wollongong, New South Wales, Australia, Jens Woelk in Trento, Italy, and John Borrows in Vancouver, Canada deserve special mention for their support and encouragement. Francesco Palermo and Alexandra Tomaselli of the European Academy of Bozen/Bolzano in northern Italy arranged a seminar in Bolzano where I presented and received invaluable suggestions on the major themes of this manuscript. In similar fashion, Eduardo Rodriguez Veltze and Ivanna Arizcurinaga organized my participation at the VIII Congreso Internacional de la Red Latinoamericana de Antropologia Juridica (RELAJU) meeting on legal pluralism in Sucre, Bolivia.

I received tremendously helpful research assistance from two of Dartmouth's brightest and most dedicated students (now alumni), Eric M. Schildge and Laura C. Sayler. I also extend thanks to the library staff at Baker Library and to the administration at Dartmouth College for their support of my research. Laura Gillen of Vermont Law School generously provided expert technical assistance in the formatting of the manuscript.

I extend warm thanks and appreciation to Jim and Susan Wright, long-time colleagues and friends from Dartmouth College. As a young faculty member at Dartmouth during the late 1960s, Jim Wright was among the first people to urge the college to revitalize its historic charter commitment for the education of American Indian students. Years later, as Dean of the Faculty, Provost, and finally, President of Dartmouth College, Jim oversaw the growth and development of Native American Studies into one of the country's strongest interdisciplinary programs in Native Studies. As a Native graduate of Dartmouth and now, as a faculty member in its Native American Studies program, I have benefitted enormously from Jim and Susan's steadfast support and activism. I am honored to dedicate this book to them, as well as to my family, as a small token of my appreciation and gratitude.

Finally, I thank my entire family for their ongoing love and support. My wife Hilde, our children Lisa, Joe, and Alanna, and our grandchildren, Zion and Aniiya, are a constant source of inspiration, love, and fun. They are the bright lights in my life.

N.B.D.

SHADOW NATIONS

Introduction

This book is concerned with the erosion of inherent tribal sovereign powers caused primarily by the legacy of imperialist federal powers that have served to move the nation away from its formative commitments to a legally plural society. It argues for ideological and institutional reforms that will help redirect the trajectory of tribal–federal relations to better reflect the formative ethos of legal pluralism that characterized intergovernmental relations in the early years of this republic. In the process, these reforms will help acknowledge and reaffirm a more robust and meaningful form of territorial sovereignty for Indian tribes.

The pathway to this end result is complicated, however, by a number of potential obstacles. First, there are considerations of *ideology*, more particularly, our national commitment to a political and legal theory and model of sovereignty that sees the nation-state and its institutions as the only legitimate sources of law. Second, there are considerations of *constitutionalism* and the limits on an otherwise expansive federal power in Indian affairs to condone or to subject US citizens (Native and non-Native) to the authority of indigenous legal systems in which they cannot participate politically and that are not directly constrained by the Constitution and the Bill of Rights. Finally, there are considerations of *institutionalism*, and more particularly, the forms of intergovernmental tribal and national relations that must be developed to better accommodate and advance the pluralistic elements contained within our formative documents, including the Constitution and the legacy of treaty-making.

The considerations of ideology complicate the pathway to the proposed reforms by interposing the dominance of the nation-state. M. B. Hooker stated the problem rather succinctly in his early study on legal pluralism: "The form of political organization within which plural legal systems exist today is the nation-state. It is fundamental to the idea of the state that its institutions alone can be the source of law. Laws are valid only in so far as they are acknowledged in some way by the organs of the state.... This may be a proper view in a culturally and economically homogeneous society, but such societies are the exception rather than the rule. An undue emphasis on this view of law is often a distortion of reality and not uncommonly a downright misrepresentation in many states."[1]

P. G. McHugh similarly states the problem but in a way that addresses the situation of indigenous peoples:

> [C]onstitutional lawyers and courts cleaving intellectually to the unitary common law model of sovereignty—itself (it will be seen) largely a nineteenth-century model—were unable to recognize a shared or multiple version. During the nineteenth century the proper treatment of aboriginal peoples had required application of the unitary and absolutist view of settler-state sovereignty. By that view, aboriginal peoples were treated as absorbed—assimilated—wholly

> into the legal system of the settler-state. This desideratum of the indigenous person becoming an individual citizen or subject, their tribal community and association dissolved, was put into laws already contemplating that result. They were predicated upon the ultimate overriding sovereignty of the *arriviste* white polity.[2]

The challenge for Indian tribes, and indigenous peoples generally, is to confront and overcome this ideology of *legal centralism*, and the overriding institutional supremacy of the nation-state. In this effort, Indian tribes and their advocates will necessarily have to confront and address as well the national commitment to liberalism, the dominant political philosophy that undergirds our liberal democracy and situates the individual, not the group or the collective, as the bedrock moral unit of society. Since these ideological challenges are manifested in a multitude of intellectual domains—historical, jurisprudential, and philosophical—a careful examination of them will necessarily take time. As a result, the first four chapters of this book are devoted to a closer examination of the diverse ideological challenges that potentially stand in the way of a more robust expression of tribal sovereignty.

The considerations of constitutionalism are actually two-fold. First, they embrace the reality that the modern court has managed to insinuate constitutional values (like liberty, representative government, equality under the law) as a vehicle to constrain the scope of inherent tribal powers, while leaving intact its long-standing view that the Constitution and the Bill of Rights do not directly apply to or constrain tribal powers. These concerns highlight the fact that any proposed ideological and institutional reforms necessarily will have to address the panoply of checks or, as Duncan Ivison calls them, "reversal points,"[3] that should be available to individuals to guard against abusive, corrupt, and/or incompetent actions of tribal governments, including but not limited to checks imposed by federal legislation like the Indian Civil Rights Act of 1968.

Second, the considerations of constitutionalism embrace concerns that there may be structural constitutional limits on the power of Congress to recognize a more robust form of tribal sovereign authority and to affirm power over all persons for all acts (including criminal offenses) committed within tribal lands. This notion of full territorial sovereignty for tribes has been expressly rejected by the modern Supreme Court through reasoning that is of dubious integrity in terms of its reading of history, legal doctrine, and philosophy. The earliest articulation of these potential constitutional limits came from Justice Anthony Kennedy who first voiced such concerns while serving as an appellate judge on the Ninth Circuit Court of Appeals. He has since refined these views as a member of the US Supreme Court. Since Justice Kennedy's ideological and jurisprudential views often place him at the center of many of the court's decisions, the proposed reforms necessarily will have to address his analysis of the structural limits on the powers of Congress to alter the status of tribal powers in the modern era. Chapter 5 is thus dedicated to a presentation of these constitutional considerations.

Finally, we must take account of considerations of *institutionalism*, or the structural forms by and through which tribal and national intergovernmental relations can operate to better accommodate and advance the pluralistic elements contained within our formative documents, including the Constitution and the legacy of treaty-making. Historically, these intergovernmental relations were conducted through a discourse of treaty-making and later, through ordinary federal legislation. In the modern era, some scholars have advocated the use of constitutional amendments as the preferred institutional medium through which to entrench protections for tribal sovereignty. Others have called for the revival of some form of treaty-making, recognizing a tripartite sovereign regime of *treaty federalism*. In chapter 6, I examine these various forms of institutional arrangements and ultimately suggest a form of bilateralism that borrows from international law and yields a model of intergovernmental relations that I call *conventions on tribal sovereignty* whose moral force is grounded in considerations of mutual respect, consent, and commitment to coexistence in shared territories.

The narratives that follow inevitably describe stories of conflict over political power—who gets to claim it, to use it, and to limit it in the hands of others. Whether we frame the normative discourse as conflicts over political ideology, the demands of constitutionalism, or institutional arrangements for intergovernmental relations, we invariably encounter a familiar and recurring national narrative—how to establish peaceful, respectful, and enduring relations between divergent societies coexisting within common territories. Situating the claims of tribal governments for more robust forms of inherent sovereign authority within the discourse of legal pluralism is, I believe, a critical step in that direction. It is an approach that requires us, as a nation of nations, to confront and address fundamental questions about the nature of legitimate government, about political power and about respect for differences among societies and individuals. The answers to those fundamental questions will help determine whether we can manage to create and respect the juridical space for legally plural societies to operate effectively within a shared territory or whether we continue to force segments of our plural society—the Indian tribal nations—to function within the shadows of the omnipresent and dominant nation-state.

CHAPTER 1

Tribal Sovereignty and Legal Pluralism

The origin story behind this project goes back to August 2008, when I wrote and published an op-ed in the *New York Times* entitled "Broken Justice." That piece helped shed light on the pernicious problem of sexual violence against Native women in Indian country. According to the US Department of Justice, the rate at which Indian women are subjected to sexual violence is 2.5 times that for other women in the United States. In addition, the data revealed that weapons are used in these violent assaults much more frequently than in cases involving non-Native women; this means that in addition to the sexual violence, Native women are at higher risk of being stabbed and/or bludgeoned with various objects. And finally, the data indicated that the perpetrators of these crimes are overwhelmingly non-Indian men, and indeed, they are mostly white men.

In the piece, I pointed out that the morass of jurisdictional rules in this area exacerbated the problem of sexual violence in Indian country. I drew attention to one case, the US Supreme

Court's 1978 opinion in *Oliphant v. Suquamish Indian Tribe*,[1] that dealt a particularly devastating blow to tribal governments and seriously compromised the efficacy of law enforcement in Indian country. *Oliphant* held that Indian tribes lacked the inherent sovereign power to prosecute non-Indian offenders for violations of tribal law. According to the court, the exercise of tribal governmental powers is constrained by the tribes' status as "domestic dependent nations" and thus, any powers inconsistent with that status are "implicitly divested." In the context of the problem of sexual violence in Indian country, the *Oliphant* decision effectively deprived the governments closest to the problem, the Indian tribes, of the opportunity to prosecute the offenders (most of whom are non-Indians). Moreover, US Department of Justice data and other studies suggest that the governments that do have jurisdiction, the federal government (or in some instances, the states), do not regularly, effectively, or consistently exercise it.[2]

Oliphant's implicit divestiture rule has since been extended into cases dealing with civil and regulatory matters,[3] and it was applied in another criminal case, *Duro v. Reina* (1990),[4] to divest tribes of authority to prosecute non-member Indian offenders. Congress acted quickly following the *Duro* decision to restore and reaffirm tribal criminal jurisdiction over nonmember Indians, but it left the *Oliphant* ruling intact.[5]

In ushering a new and extraordinarily lethal legal doctrine into the mix, the *Oliphant* decision transformed the nature of litigation and advocacy in Indian country by elevating challenges to the *exercise* of tribal power into challenges about the very *existence* of tribal power. The decision positions the courts, as opposed to the Congress, as the principal arbiter of the scope of tribal powers using a rather standardless metric that assesses the legitimacy of tribal powers in light of their conformity with an imposed status as "domestic dependent nations." As such, *Oliphant* stands as the Court's most significant and controversial Indian law decision of the modern era. In the op-ed, I urged Congress legislatively to overrule the decision and reaffirm the tribes' full territorial sovereignty over all offenders in Indian country, Indian and non-Indian alike. Even then, I recognized that this formulation of tribal sovereignty pressed on the prevailing conceptions of tribal sovereignty and general notions of legal pluralism that typically tolerated the application of tribal law in intragroup settings but rarely envisioned that law reaching nonmembers, especially in criminal matters.

The op-ed triggered a number of responses on the *New York Times*' website, most of which were highly sympathetic to the problems I highlighted and to the proposal I advanced. But quite a few responses took issue with my call for placing greater power over these matters into the hands of tribal governments. The concerns ran the gamut from corrupt and/or incompetent tribal leaders to pseudo-historical claims that "Indians lost the war" and should "get over it." One writer offered the following commentary that is particularly germane to this project:

> The problem highlighted is real and troublesome, but the remedy suggested is foolish and misguided. What are needed are the dissolution of separate jurisdiction, and the enforcement of State and Federal jurisdiction on tribal lands and members. Having race-based enclaves where there is no equal protection of the law is simply intolerable in a pluralistic, democratic society. We Americans are one people, regardless of racial background. We should have one law. The trouble is that we have tribal governance in the first place, not that tribal governance is limited. Having local governments of the people, for the people, and by the people, with equal protection for everyone, and under the umbrella of State and Federal law is the answer. Putting justice into the hands of corrupt casino-tribal governments and their BIA lackeys is not.[6]

Besides inviting a new round of termination of tribal political status,[7] this writer's critique implicitly embraces what John Griffiths calls the "ideology of legal centralism," the view that "law is and should be the law of the state, uniform for all persons, exclusive of all other law, and administered by a single set of state institutions. To the extent that other, lesser normative orderings, such as the church, the family, the voluntary association and the economic organization exist, they ought to be and in fact are hierarchically subordinate to the law and institutions of the state."[8] Pursuant to the ideology of legal centralism, all other systems of normative ordering (whether they produce what is properly called "law" or not) are subordinate to and subsist within the shadows of the nation-state. In his earlier writings, M. B. Hooker also drew attention to the asserted positional supremacy of the state in relation to all other forms of social ordering. According to Hooker, "It is fundamental to the idea of the state that its institutions alone can be the source of law. Laws are valid only in so far as they are acknowledged in some way by the organs of the state. The law is defined, in other words, as a set of consistent principles, valid for and binding upon the whole population and emanating from a single source. The written, rational state system is the only one which is 'properly law'."[9]

Importantly, both Hooker and Griffiths challenge the central proposition advanced by the ideology of legal centralism. They argue instead that most societies in the world are characterized by forms of legal pluralism, where "multiple systems of legal obligation" exist within a particular state.[10] In a similar vein, Stephen Tierney has called attention to the reality of "plurinational" states in various parts of the world and to the persistence of "discrete *demoi*" who advocate for new and more robust forms of recognition from and within the state. Tierney focuses his attention on Catalonia/

Spain, Quebec/Canada, and Scotland/United Kingdom but the strategic moves made by these "sub-state territorial polities" for greater recognition by the state have important parallels to and implications for American Indian tribes. Like the tribes in the United States, the societies Tierney considers "position themselves in a relational way to the state not as internal 'minorities', but rather as polities which are in fact comparable to the state in the way they offer, or have the potential to offer, an effective site for many if not all of those functional and identificatory roles which the state plays in the life of the citizens."[11] Such strategic moves challenge the "monists" or adherents to the ideology of legal centralism to revise or reconceptualize their notions of the state or nation. In Tierney's words, "those who adhere to the traditional conceptualisation of the 'nation-state' as one politico-constitutional territory encapsulating a unitary national society are charged with the task of reconceiving the plurinational state in appreciation of its essential societal plurality."[12]

Indeed, the traditional conceptualization of the "nation-state" as described by Tierney is itself something of a late arrival in the evolution of western legal systems. Put another way, as noted by Hooker and Griffiths above, it is legal pluralism, not legal centralism, that has often served as a predominate feature of western forms of government. Canadian constitutional scholar Roderick MacDonald offers this perspective on legal pluralism in relation to the rise of the "monistic" nation-state:

> [L]egal pluralism is not novel. Until the seventeenth century in Europe the idea of a territorial State (later associated more with blood than with geography in the phrase 'nation-state') claiming an exclusive capacity to regulate everyday activity would have been thought bizarre. Neither the Romans (with, *inter alia*, their conceptions of *jus civile* and *jus gentium*) nor the medieval kings

> of England (who tolerated both customary law of the realm and of localities, and divergent manorial, ecclesiastical and mercantile legal systems) claimed a monopoly on law and normativity. What is more, even into the nineteenth century, the legal and political *elites* of England and France, for example, did not see law as singular. That is, only with codification on the continent and with the *Judicature Acts* in common law jurisdictions did the image of a single, State- managed legal system begin to emerge.[13]

The social contexts in which legal pluralism is seen to operate have not remained static over the years. As Paul Schiff Berman explains, "legal pluralists have sought to document hybrid legal spaces, where more than one legal, or quasi-legal, regime occupies the same social field. Historically, such sites were most prominently associated either with colonialism—where the legal system imposed by empire was layered on top of indigenous legal systems—or the study of religion—where canon law and other spiritual codes have often existed in an uneasy relationship with the state legal system."[14] The study of legal pluralism in the context of colonial societies and the attendant encounters between Indigenous peoples and European imperialists are particularly attentive to and concerned with the interactions of these respective legal systems in conditions of grossly unequal power. Sally Engle Merry refers to this as "classic legal pluralism."[15] In contrast, what she calls the "new legal pluralism" describes inquiries into legal relations within modern industrial nations that embrace a wider variety of social ordering forms besides state law that largely "operate in its shadows." But even in these contexts, Merry acknowledges the preponderant role that the state's legal apparatus has in relation to these other forms of social regulation.[16] In both contexts, it seems apparent that the legal pluralist is intensely interested in identifying the forms of normative ordering, including legal systems, that have meaning to the socially plural societies occupying the same social field and examining the operation of those normative ordering systems in relation to the power of the state.[17]

What precisely constitutes a "legal system" and "law" is, of course, a subject of considerable interest and debate among scholars from various disciplines, including legal anthropologists, political scientists, sociologists, and traditional legal scholars. The social anthropologists, Franz and Keebet von Benda-Beckmann, offer the following definition of "legal system":

> The most visible kind of plural legal constellation is the co-existence of two or more legal systems. By 'legal systems' we mean a body of legal rules and regulations conceived of as a totality and represented as a bounded symbolic universe by social actors, and for which often, but not necessarily, a claim of internal systematisation and coherence is made. Such orders provide substantive and procedural rules and principles for social, economic, political organisation, and usually also constitute persons or organisations as legitimate authorities for solving problems with the help of these conceptions.[18]

American Indian tribes have long been regarded in US law as possessing and operating legal systems that accord with this definition. In its seminal decision in *Cherokee Nation v. Georgia* (1831), the US Supreme Court described the political status of Indian tribes in the following language:

> So much of the argument as was intended to prove the character of the Cherokees as a state, as a distinct political society, separated from others, capable of managing its own affairs and governing itself, has, in the opinion of a majority of the judges, been completely successful.[19]

To be sure, *Cherokee Nation* also described tribes as "domestic dependent nations," whose relationship to the United States "resembles that of a ward to his guardian."[20] It is important, however, to understand the ideological context in which the court so characterized the political status of tribes. The court's language of dependency and protectionism was rooted in principles of intergovernmental relations derived from international law. This understanding is derived from the dissenting opinion in *Cherokee Nation* of Justice Smith Thompson who, along with Justice Joseph Story, wrote the opinion at the suggestion of Chief Justice John Marshall. The dissenting opinion was announced just over a week after the court's decision in the case. According to Justice Story, "neither Judge T. or myself contemplated delivering a dissenting opinion [in *Cherokee Nation v. Georgia*] until the Chief Justice suggested to us the propriety of it, and his own desire that we should do it."[21] In their dissenting opinion, Justices Thompson and Story described the nature of the tribes' political relationship with the United States in the following terms:

> The terms *state* and *nation* are used in the law of nations, as well as in common parlance, as importing the same thing; and imply a body of men, united together, to procure their mutual safety and advantage by means of their union.... We ought, therefore, to reckon in the number of sovereigns those states that have bound themselves to another more powerful, although by an unequal alliance. The conditions of these unequal alliances may be infinitely varied; but whatever they are, provided the inferior ally reserves to itself the sovereignty or the right to govern its own body, it ought to be considered an independent state. Consequently, a weak state, that, in order to provide for its safety, places itself under the protection of a more powerful one, without stripping itself of the right of government and sovereignty, does not cease on this account to be placed among the sovereigns who acknowledge no other power. Tributary and feudatory states do not thereby cease to be

> sovereign and independent states, so long as self government, and sovereign and independent authority is left in the administration of the state. Vattel, c. 1, pp. 16, 17.[22]

The very next year, in *Worcester v. Georgia* (1832), Chief Justice Marshall relied on substantially the same language in reaffirming the national character of Indian tribes and describing tribal relations with the United States as "that of a nation claiming and receiving the protection of one more powerful; not that of individuals abandoning their national character, and submitting as subjects to the laws of a master."[23] According to Marshall, the national government viewed the Indian tribes as "distinct political communities, having territorial boundaries, within which their authority is exclusive, and having a right to all the lands within those boundaries, which is not only acknowledged, but guarantied by the United States."[24]

As noted by the Supreme Court in the *Cherokee* cases, the language of the Constitution itself, along with the long course of treaty making with European nations, and later, with the United States, provide further grounding for the view of tribes as separate and distinct polities. Article I, section 8 of the Constitution assigns to Congress the exclusive power to "regulate Commerce with foreign Nations, and among the several States, and with the Indian Tribes." The documentary history on the evolution of this clause provides important insight into the drafters' understanding of tribal societies and their constitutional relationship with the emerging national government. At the Constitutional Convention of 1787, the initial draft of the commerce clause power made no reference to Indian tribes. On August 18, 1787, James Madison submitted language to the Committee of Detail, which added the following language to the list of powers belonging to the "General Legislature": "to regulate affairs with the Indians as well within as without the limits of the U. States."[25] On September 4, 1787, the drafting committee recommended a series of amendments to the Convention, including a proposal to add "and with the Indian Tribes" to the extant commerce clause.[26] It is critical to note the shift in language from regulating "affairs with the Indians" to "regulating commerce ... with the Indian Tribes." The final language approved by the framers constitutionalized a tripartite regime of political relationships between the national government in Congress and three distinct polities—foreign nations, states, and Indian Tribes. Tribes were conceptualized as discrete polities, occupying a sphere of authority and sovereignty on par with foreign nations and the states. Equally significant is the framers' choice of relational language that empowers Congress to regulate commerce "with," not "of," the Indian tribes. This suggests that the framers contemplated that there were textual, and perhaps even structural, limits on the power of Congress to manage political relations with the Indian tribes.

Robert N. Clinton, perhaps the foremost constitutional historian of tribal-federal-state relations, has written extensively about this period of American constitutional history. He affirms that the framers of the Indian Commerce Clause had three principal purposes in mind. First, they intended to provide for exclusive federal authority in regulating commerce with the Indian tribes, to the exclusion of the states. Second, they intended to nullify any claims to residual state authority over Indian affairs that stemmed from Article XI of the Articles of Confederation, which, in pertinent part, provided: "The United States in Congress assembled, shall also have the sole and exclusive right and power of regulating the trade and managing all affairs with the Indians not members of any of the states; provided that the legislative right of any State within its own limits be not infringed or violated." Finally, they intended to accord protection for the Indian tribes in their capacity as sovereign political entities. In Clinton's words, "the framers' determination to protect the sovereignty of the Indian tribes as peoples separate from the states was evident in their enumeration among the states and foreign nations in the Commerce Clause and in the apportionment formula which excluded Indians not taxed."[27]

Clinton's scholarship also affirms that the framers and other national leaders during the early American period understood the federal power in Indian affairs to be limited, constrained both by the textual language of the Constitution and by shared understandings of the legacy of treaty-making that pre-dated the formation of the union. One of the clearest exemplars of this understanding was revealed in the debates surrounding the federal Removal Act of 1830[28] that authorized the president of the United States, after obtaining the consent of the tribes, to negotiate for the exchange of tribal lands in the east for lands in the Indian Territory (present-day Oklahoma). To rebut suggestions that Indian tribes were subject to unilateral (as opposed to bilateral) federal power, a member of Congress introduced an 1814 letter from John Quincy Adams, Henry Clay, and others responding to earlier British charges about American overreaching in its management of Indian affairs:

> Under [the United States constitutional] system, the Indians residing within the United States are so far independent that they live under their own customs, *and not under the laws of the United States*; that their rights upon the lands where they inhabit or hunt are secured to them by boundaries defined in amicable treaties between the United States and themselves; and that whenever those boundaries are varied, it is also by amicable and voluntary treaties, by which they receive from the United States ample compensation for every right they have to the lands ceded by them.[29]

Toward the latter part of the nineteenth century, the Supreme Court reaffirmed the status of Indian tribes as autonomous sovereign bodies. In *Talton v. Mayes* (1896), the court held that tribal powers were local powers of self-government that were not constrained by the US Constitution, although paradoxically "subject to its general provisions and the paramount authority of congress."[30] Given the tribes' status as pre-constitutional political bodies, the court's holding that tribes were also "extra-constitutional" was not particularly surprising. The genuine surprise was the court's reaffirmation of tribal sovereignty at a time when federal policy had turned decidedly against tribal interests and in favor of an assimilationist agenda that aimed to eradicate communal Indian land holdings and, indeed, Indian culture itself.

From this brief historical perspective, the constitutional dimensions of the tribal–federal relationship reveal a shared understanding about the cultural, and more importantly, political distinctiveness of tribal polities in relation to their federal (and state) counterparts. Far from incorporating the citizens of the tribal nations into the emerging national *demos* of the Constitution's "We the People," early American leaders contemplated the formation of a plurinational state, whereby tribal governments and the national government would engage in political discourse via the medium of negotiated treaties. President George Washington insisted that treaties with Indian tribes adhere to the same formalities as treaties with foreign nations in requiring the formal approval of the US Senate.[31] Conceptually, then, the national origin story is one of legal pluralism, where tribal legal systems and the newly emerging federal-state legal system were intended to coexist within the same social fields.

This formative notion of plurinationalism within the emerging United States resonates well with indigenous models for intersocietal and intergovernmental relationships that date back to the colonial era. The Haudenosaunee or tribes of the Iroquois Confederacy developed a framework for peaceful coexistence of multiple nations sharing common territories. Their Great Law of Peace was based on the principle of respect for the distinctive culture and national autonomy of other societies. This ethic of intergovernmental respect was the cornerstone for the confederacy's model of traditional diplomacy, expressed through a ceremonial beaded wampum belt known as the *Kaswentha* or the "Two Row Wampum." The Kaswentha was the embodiment of a Haudenosaunee political philosophy on the proper model for achieving peaceful intersocietal coexistence in shared territories. Mohawk political scientist Taiaiake Alfred offers this perspective on the Kaswentha:

> The Kanien'kehaka [or Mohawk] Kaswentha (Two-Row Wampum) principle embodies this notion of power in the context of relations between nations. Instead of subjugating one to the other, the Kanien'kehaka who opened their territory to Dutch traders in the early seventeenth century negotiated an original and lasting peace based on coexistence of power in a context of respect for the autonomy and distinctive nature of each partner. The metaphor for this relationship—two vessels, each possessing its own integrity, traveling the river of time together—was conveyed visually on a wampum belt of two parallel purple lines (representing power) on a background of white beads (representing peace). In this respectful (co-equal) friendship and alliance, any interference with the other partner's autonomy, freedom, or powers was expressly forbidden. So long as these principles were respected, the relationship would be peaceful, harmonious, and just.[32]

In the present-day era of tribal self-determination, this formative ethos of legal pluralism is still evident, but it operates in severely muted or diminished forms.[33] From the lens of classic legal pluralism, we can see that the contemporary relationship between Indian tribes and the federal government reflects a palpable structural imbalance of power, the product of the colonial experience and the United States' own imperialism into Indian country (and beyond) throughout the late nineteenth and early twentieth centuries. During this period, federal policy in Indian affairs unleashed a variety of forces—military, social, religious, biological, and economic—that played a significant role in diminishing tribal populations, severing their historic connections to ancestral homelands, and systematically assaulting tribal identity and indigenous cultural integrity.[34] The federal government's allotment policy, in operation from the late 1880s into the 1930s, was particularly effective in drastically reducing the land holdings of tribes in favor of non-Indian homesteaders; Indian lands dropped from 138 million acres to about 48 million acres during this period.[35] Equally significant, the policy led to the massive influx of white, Christian settlers into those residual pockets of Indian country that survived the allotment process. The radical shifts in the sociodemographic profile of Indian country laid the foundation for the eventual encroachment of state law into Indian territories and for the gradual weakening of tribal systems of self-governance over individuals and activities occurring within tribal homelands.

From the lens of both the classic and the "new" legal pluralism, we can also track a long and sustained ideological assault by national (and state) officials and policy makers on tribal sovereignty, a phenomenon that is the particular concern of this project and the subject of much of the next chapter. Often working in parallel with the sociohistorical forces that led to the diminishment of tribal populations, loss of tribal lands, and the attempted eradication of tribal culture and Indian identity, the ideological assault on tribal sovereignty was manifested in legislative acts and judicial pronouncements that radically altered and circumscribed the nature and scope of tribal political authority, particularly over nonmembers of the tribes, to the point where the very existence of tribes as jurisgenerative or law-producing political bodies has been called into serious question. In 1871, for example, Congress unilaterally legislated an end to treaty making with Indian tribes, a move that presaged a reconceptualization of tribal sovereignty and tilted the arc of federal Indian policy toward unilateral and self-serving legislation, and away from bilateral, negotiated, and constitutionally sanctioned treaty agreements.[36] In the year before this legislation was enacted, Lewis Downing, the Cherokee Nation's principal chief, wrote to the Board of Indian Commissioners to register his concerns about what he saw as the increasing "domestication" of federal Indian policy:

> We are told it would make no difference how we are secured and protected, so it is effected; and that it can be done as effectually by legislation as by treaty. But to us it appears that when once cut loose from our treaty moorings, we will roll and tumble upon the tempestuous ocean of American politics and congressional legislation, and shipwreck will be our inevitable destination. We now have our moorings—we have the protection of this powerful Government to look to—its pledges to rely upon; need we apologize for thinking that the Government of Washington and the Adamses is still generous and honorable?[37]

Chief Downing appreciated both the ideological and the practical effects of a shift in federal–tribal relations that would cut tribes loose from "their treaty moorings." From an ideological perspective, the move signaled a diminishment in the tribe's sovereign character in the sense that intergovernmental relations with the national government would proceed as a matter of national domestic policy. From a practical perspective, the shift away from treaty making left tribes vulnerable to the vicissitudes of federal policies shaped principally by national values and interests, with minimal or no regard for the welfare or interests of tribal governments.

The constitutionality of the 1871 law was called into serious question by several members of the Congress that enacted it and subsequently by noted scholars in the field of federal Indian law and, more recently, by at least one contemporary member of the US Supreme Court.[38] In his concurring opinion in *United States v. Lara* (2004), Associate Justice Clarence Thomas wrote the following: "In 1871, Congress enacted a statute that purported to prohibit entering into treaties with the 'Indian nation[s] or tribe[s]'. Although this Act is constitutionally suspect, (the Constitution vests in the President both the power to make treaties, Art. II, 2, cl. 2, and to recognize foreign governments, Art. II, 3) it nevertheless reflects the view of the political branches that the tribes had become a purely domestic matter" (citations omitted).[39]

This national impulse to suppress or diminish the nature and scope of tribal authority, and by extension the formative ethos of legal pluralism, continues today, albeit in more oblique strategic moves. In December 2010, the United States became the last western industrialized nation to sign onto the United Nations Declaration on the Rights of Indigenous Peoples adopted in September 2007. The Declaration affirms the right of indigenous peoples to self-determination and provides that by virtue of that right, "they freely determine their political status and freely pursue their economic, social and cultural development."[40] In other provisions, the Declaration provides for the "free, prior and informed consent" of indigenous peoples before certain state action may be imposed upon them, including state action that may lead to the removal of indigenous peoples from their lands or territories or state legislation or other rules that may affect them.[41] In its statement announcing its support of the Declaration, the United States managed to dilute, if not completely eviscerate, the rights afforded by the Declaration. For example, the United States characterized the Declaration's right of self-determination as a "new and distinct international concept of self-determination *specific to indigenous peoples*" and "different from the existing right of self-determination in international law" before lending its support (emphasis added).[42] The qualification was to underscore the United States' view that Indian tribes were not "peoples" in the international law sense of the term or otherwise recognized and functioning as fully autonomous states. This application of a *sui generis* conception of the tribes' inherent powers of self-government echoes the nation's nineteenth-century application of a *sui generis* conception of *Indian title* to property. The latter doctrine was derived from the controversial and racialized doctrine of discovery that effectively deprived tribes of ownership interests in their lands because of their status as savage infidels, leaving them with a residual right of occupancy completely subject to the whim of the sovereign and terminable without compensation.[43] As for the requirements for "free, prior and informed consent," the United States again qualified its understanding of the Declaration's provisions before issuing its support. According to its signing statement, the United States "recognizes the significance of the Declaration's provisions on free, prior and informed consent, which [it] understands to call for a process of meaningful consultation with tribal leaders, *but not necessarily the agreement of those leaders*, before the actions addressed in those consultations are taken" (emphasis added).[44] In other words, the United States substituted a right of consultation for a right of informed consent so as not to hinder or impair national (or state) action that might negatively impact on otherwise protected tribal interests that are now explicitly addressed by the UN Declaration.

To this point, we can already discern that the course of tribal sovereignty did not evolve along the lines that Native peoples likely contemplated and comprehended, or along the trajectory suggested by the early commitments to intersocietal political coexistence between the tribes and the national government. In other words, the history of tribal–federal political relations reveals an early and quite radical break from what I have called the formative ethos of legal pluralism. Why and how did this occur? And just as importantly, is it possible or even desirable to recapture that formative ethos in the modern-day political arrangements between tribes and the national government? Or are Indian tribes destined to operate, if at all, within the shadows of an omnipresent, and often repressive and paternal, national polity? These are the questions to which we turn in the next chapters.

CHAPTER 2

In the Shadows of the Nation-State

The seeds of ambivalence about the place of Indian tribes in our constitutional democracy were planted almost at the beginning of our national creation story. In 1787, *The American Museum*, the nation's first monthly magazine, published the full text of the Constitution as part of the ratification debate. In the same year, and in the same bound annual volume, the magazine also published literary works that signaled the demise of Indian people. As Renee L. Bergland observed, "In public discourse, the birth of the American nation and the death of the Native American were as closely related as light and shadow."[1] The literary works included Philip Freneau's 1787 poem, "Lines Occasioned by a visit to an old Indian Burying Ground," or more commonly, "The Indian Burying Ground." In the poem's last verse, the writer "conjures up spectral Natives ... [and] brings forth the doubts and regrets that haunt the American project":[2]

> And long shall timorous fancy see
> The painted chief, and pointed spear,

And reason's self shall bow the knee
To shadows and delusions here.[3]

The union of narratives about one nation's emergence and another's imminent demise was a significant ideological move toward the formation of a national identity, a move that worked in the opposite direction of, or at least in tension with, the formative ethos of legal pluralism. As Bergland states, "It is particularly noteworthy that Freneau's archetypal poem, 'The Indian Burying Ground', and the federal Constitution were both first published in the 1787 volume of *The American Museum*. This coincidence of publication gives an indication of both documents' importance to the construction of American nationhood, particularly since, as Benedict Anderson argues, nationalism itself derived in great measure from the pamphlets, broadsheets, newspapers, and magazines that unified their readers into an 'imagined political community'."[4]

This chapter will explore the role that the construction of America's "imagined political community" played in catalyzing the nation's impulse to empire in Indian country while simultaneously repressing the formative ethos of legal pluralism. The focus, though not an exclusive one, will be on highlighting the ideological moves that signaled the elevation of the emerging nation-state and the concomitant suppression or diminishment of the tribal nations. We will begin with a closer look at the tensions that inhere between pluralism and conceptions of a "people" or "nation." Here, the work of William E. Connolly will be of particular interest and focus. In the next chapter, we will examine the challenges posed by our dual commitments to liberalism and to legal pluralism in the context of tribal sovereignty. Finally, in chapter 4, we will trace the ideological "morphing" of entrenched concepts within the body of federal Indian law, in particular the concepts of "incorporation" and "dependency," to reveal how the operation of tribal–federal relations moved from a horizontal axis of bilateralism, animated by notions of mutuality and respect for the dignity and autonomy of Indian nations, to a more vertical axis of unilateralism, animated by notions of dominance and intolerance for indigenous cultural and political differences.

William E. Connolly, one of the leading scholars of pluralist thought, has written eloquently about the risks to vulnerable minorities posed by the drive for national unity. The collateral damage from such homogenizing forces, according to Connolly, exacerbates, rather than ameliorates, the existing inequalities that persist in American society. He writes:

> Under contemporary conditions of rapid mobility within and between states, the drive to national unit itself too readily fosters marginalization of vulnerable minorities. It does so because the rapid pace of late-modern life—the rapid movement of populations, ideas, technologies, identities, and faiths across generations and territorial borders works against the realization of the national imaginary. So when an effort is made to mobilize public support for the reduction of economic inequality, vocal nationalists on the Right argue against these drives on the grounds, first, that many whom they demean would be included among their beneficiaries and, second, that the programs would undermine fixed capitalist principles undergirding the nation. National health care? That would cover welfare recipients, unwed mothers, and (usually in code language) racial minorities. It would also obstruct the free market. The provision of collective goods to help households make ends meet in the domains of transportation, housing, education, and insurance? These policies would subsidize lazy freeloaders in the cities and undermine the untrammeled free enterprise system around which the nation is built.[5]

The inclination toward unitarianism will continue to constrain and suppress diversity until we embrace what Connolly calls "deep, multidimensional pluralism," or in other words, an expansive disposition toward diversity in a wide range of interpersonal and intersocietal relations and sites of activity. For Connolly, the critical issue is "the kind of ethos infused into a doctrine or creed. What counts is how the relational dispositions of people blend into the creeds and philosophies that they embrace and the quality of the institutional ethos of engagement between partisans of different kinds."[6] In relation to sovereignty, this means that we ought to pay close attention to "the constitutive tension between the already established pattern of diversity and the periodic eruption of new constituencies seeking a place on the register of legitimacy," as well as to the "multiple *sites* of potential citizen action within and above the state" (emphasis in original).[7] Connolly's framework strives to build upon, not resist, the multivalent interests of society as expressed through the medium of "majority assemblages" rather than an imagined unified nation. The result, he writes, is "more analogous to a potluck supper than a formal dinner,"[8] where the participants assume responsibility for and play an active role in the creation, design, and implementation of the shared communal activity. The critical animating force within such sites is what Connolly calls "an ethos of critical responsiveness to new social movements, an ethos that opens up cultural space through which new possibilities of being might be enacted."[9] Although Connolly does not use the term, the ethos of critical responsiveness hinges on the adoption of a posture of humility about the "rightness" of one's beliefs and values and a consciousness regarding one's disposition toward diversity. Most crucially for Connolly, the ethos of critical responsiveness is *self-revisionary* in the sense that it may require change for those whose social positioning is contingent upon the repression of others. For Connolly, "[c]ritical responsiveness to the injuries of Otherness (e.g., to Indians, atheists, slaves, pagans, homosexuals, ladies, illegal immigrants) implies a comparative denaturalization and reconfiguration of hegemonic identities whose character depended on these specifications of difference."[10] In response to critics who contend that such concessions to pluralism will lead to divisive fragmentation, Connolly readily admits that some differentiation along certain lines will be inevitable. But in a culture of multidimensional pluralism, such differentiation can occur without the attendant stigmatization or assigned immorality or abnormality that so often operates in the unitarian framework. In short, to pluralize "is not to fragmentize. To dogmatize is to fragmentize."[11]

There are, of course, numerous obstacles standing in the way of achieving or realizing this ethos of multidimensional plurality, chief among them, the pervasiveness and power of boundaries. "Boundaries abound," according to Connolly. They exist, or are imagined to exist, between "humanity and the gods. Between human and animal. Between life and death. Between genders, nations, peoples, times, races, classes, and territories.... Boundaries form indispensable protections against violation and violence; but the divisions they sustain also carry cruelty and violence. Boundaries provide preconditions of identity, individual agency, and collective action; but they also close off possibilities of being that might otherwise flourish. Boundaries both foster and inhibit freedom; they both protect and violate life."[12]

Connolly examines the function of boundaries in the context of people establishing claims to particular territories: "to be free you must belong to a people; to be a people you must have a common identity burned into you; to be a flourishing people you must exclusively inhabit a contiguous territory; to flourish freely as a territorialized people you must stringently define and exclude the foreign. Wandering and plurality must be repressed along a variety of dimensions."[13] He suggests that the people forming this "civi-territorial complex" operate according to a presumed and professed consentience about core mores and values. This consentience, expressed in notions of a shared culture, operates at the subterranean level to bind the people together. As such, it can tolerate fairly shallow manifestations of pluralism to the extent that the new or different expressions do not impinge upon or threaten the core, fundamental superstructure of the society.

From the perspective of this imagined landscape, Connolly examines the situation of Native peoples, building upon Alexis de Tocqueville's observations about indigenous–American relations in the early nineteenth century and the nature of American sovereignty as it relates to the tribes. Connolly writes:

> According to Tocqueville, the ethos infusing American sovereignty in the nineteenth century was above all agriculture and a Protestant, Christian tradition. That is why Amerindians could not be included in the new settler society, regardless of what the positional sovereign asserted. So when a Supreme Court decision ratified the autonomy of the Cherokee people in the Southeast, a sovereign ethos of Christian superiority personified by settler vigilante groups and the refusal by President Jackson to enforce the decision overwhelmed the positional supremacy of the Court. The irresistible demand that European stock and Christian belief provide the basis of the Republic overturned the positional authority of the Court.[14]

In this view, the Supreme Court's affirmation of the tribe's sovereign national character in the *Cherokee Nation* cases, and by extension, its validation of an ethos of legal pluralism, struck too closely to the foundational superstructure of the civi-territorial complex and ultimately was rejected by the multitude. This reveals the truth of what Connolly observes about sovereignty and American pluralism: "In the new American pluralism … sovereignty circulates uncertainly between the will of the people and the civi-theo-territorial complex that constitutes them. For 'the people' can be officially sovereign in America only because those human beings who diverge from the essence of civilization have been displaced from the land they previously wandered over and because the territorialization of civilization itself sets the parameters of popular sovereignty."[15] Connolly's views about the excesses of majoritarianism as an expression of popular sovereignty echo similar concerns expressed by James Madison in the late eighteenth century. In a 1788 letter to Thomas Jefferson, Madison explained why he was initially disinclined to support a bill of rights in the Constitution:

> Repeated violations of these parchment barriers have been committed by overbearing majorities in every state. In Virginia I have seen the bill of rights violated in every instance where it has been opposed to a popular current. Notwithstanding the explicit provision contained in that instrument for the rights of conscience, it is well known that a religious establishment would have taken place in that state if the legislative majority had found, as they expected, a majority of the people in favor of the measure; … Wherever the real power in a government lies, there is the danger of oppression. In our governments the real power lies in the majority of the community, and the invasion of private rights is *chiefly* to be apprehended, not from acts of government contrary to the sense of its constituents, but from acts in which the government is the mere instrument of the major number of the constituents. (emphasis in original)[16]

According to Madison, the security for civil rights "must be the same as for religious rights. It consists in the one case in the multiplicity of interests and, in the other, in the multiplicity of sects. The degree of security in both cases will depend on the number of interests and sects, and this may be presumed to depend on the extent of country and number of people comprehended under the same government."[17]

The nineteenth-century national imaginary constructed a national narrative organized around the foundations of agrarianism and Protestantism that allowed policy makers, as the instrument of majoritarian will, to displace American Indians or minimally, dismiss their claims for protection of their lands and their rights to self-government. In much the same fashion, the late twentieth- and early twenty-first-century national imaginary has constructed a national narrative organized around equal rights and opportunity for all, and where individual merit and achievement, not membership in a group, are the defining values. Once again, Indian tribes and their legal claims for protection of lands and rights of self-governance are placed ideologically on the "other" side of the boundary lines, where they subsist precariously at the whim of majoritarian control.

A recent study by Jeffrey Dudas shows how contemporary anti-treaty-rights activists in America have effectively exploited the discourse of rights to contest the legal claims of American Indians as undeserved "special rights." They have done this by characterizing American Indian treaty rights as antithetical to foundational American values like equal protection and equal opportunity. According to Dudas, these activists "emphasize that treaty rights conflict with the nation's commitment to protecting the equal rights of all citizens. Convinced by their special-rights talk that they are heroic defenders of an endangered American way of life, anti-treaty-rights activists construct for themselves a virtuous, and exceedingly consequential, identity as 'countersubversives' who protect the body politic from the irresponsible activism of Indians."[18] An excerpt from the editorial page of *Outdoor Life* illustrates the anti-treaty-rights rhetorical strategy:

> We have been warned by friends to lay off the Indian problem. They have cautioned ... that 'The Great American Guilty Conscience,' actively kept alive by the Indians, has stripped the American people of their ability to deal logically with the rampant Indian excesses that are becoming more flagrant every day. Make no mistake. The tribes are on the move. They aim to lay claim to as much land—your land—as they can get. **Sixty million outdoor sportspeople, countless nature lovers, and the American people in general can go to hell**.
>
> At this time, the problems are mostly in the Northern and Western states, but no state is safe. [Since] the Boldt decision in Washington State, the problem has exploded everywhere.
>
> **It is time to end our treaties with the Indians.** Indians should just be Americans like everyone else, not super Americans with special privileges. It's up to you. Now is the time to unite. Otherwise, we might yet give this country back to the Indians.[19]

Not surprisingly, the rise of these New Right anti-treaty-rights activists coincides with the renaissance of tribal activism and with America's revitalized commitment to tribal sovereignty beginning in the early 1970s. One of the most significant cases from this era, *McClanahan v. Arizona State Tax Commission* (1973) provided the occasion for the Supreme Court to take stock of tribal-federal relations over the course of the decades since the era of the *Cherokee Nation* cases.[20] Writing for a unanimous Court, Justice Thurgood Marshall's opinion acknowledged the continuing force and legacy of tribal sovereignty: "It must always be remembered that the various Indian tribes were once independent and sovereign nations, and that their claim to sovereignty long predates that of our own Government."[21] At the same time, however, the Court acknowledged that the concept of tribal sovereignty, as well as relations among the tribes, the states, and the federal government, had evolved significantly over the years in response to changing federal Indian policies and the substantially altered geopolitical and sociodemographic landscape in Indian country. The presence of large numbers of non-Indians in Indian country, for example, served as justification for the intrusion of state law into tribal communities and a concomitant diminishment in the preemptive power of tribal sovereignty within their juridical spaces. In one of *McClanahan*'s most famous passages, the Court summarized these developments in the following language: "[T]he trend has been away from the idea of inherent Indian sovereignty as a bar to state jurisdiction and toward reliance on federal pre-emption. The modern cases thus tend to avoid reliance on platonic notions of Indian sovereignty and to look instead to the applicable treaties and statutes which define the limits of state power."[22]

Justice Marshall's reference to "platonic notions of Indian sovereignty" may well have reflected his sense that the concept of tribal sovereignty, as a practical matter, had limited utility in shoring up tribal claims to power within their lands, especially in the face of unrelenting encroachment by state governments. Tribal sovereignty is still relevant in the modern era but only as a "backdrop against which the applicable treaties and federal statutes must be read."[23] From an ideological perspective, the Court's analysis regards tribal sovereignty as akin to the shadows cast upon the walls of the cave in Plato's famous allegory, an amorphous and incomplete version of the authority possessed by "true" sovereigns.[24] Indeed, the Court offered a refreshingly candid admission that its understanding, and perhaps that of the entire nation, of the place of Indian tribes within our constitutional democracy was no more advanced now than in prior centuries: "[I]t is nonetheless still true, as it was in the last century, that '[t]he relation of Indian tribes living within the borders of the United States ... [is] an anomalous one and of a complex character'."[25]

As in the *Cherokee Nation* cases, the substantive issue in *McClanahan* focused on the applicability of state law in Indian country and, in particular, whether Arizona's income tax laws could be applied to a tribal member and reservation resident whose entire income was earned on the reservation. In finding against the state, the Court rightly considered whether tribal members, at the time of treaty-making with the federal government, ever expected state law to apply within their territory. While the Court's holding ultimately preserved a measure of juridical autonomy for tribes and their members, and by extension, demonstrated some allegiance to the formative ethos of legal pluralism, the Court took pains to note that tribal expectations based on their understanding of treaty rights should be viewed in the context of their relationship with and their dependency upon the federal government:

> It is circumstances such as these which have led this Court in interpreting Indian treaties, to adopt the general rule that '[d]oubtful expressions are to be resolved in favor of the weak and defenseless people who are the wards of the nation, dependent upon its protection and good faith.' When this canon of construction is taken together with the tradition of Indian independence described above, it cannot be doubted that the reservation of certain lands for the exclusive use and occupancy of the Navajos and the exclusion of non-Navajos from the prescribed area was meant to establish the lands as within the exclusive sovereignty of the Navajos *under general federal supervision*. (emphasis added; citations omitted)[26]

On this reading, the result in *McClanahan* represented a tolerable aberration to the demands of national unity, since the limits of tribal legal pluralism were tightly circumscribed by and subject to the overarching paternal gaze and control of the federal government. As such, the case represents an exemplar of shallow pluralism where a measure of tribal independence is allowed to persist, even at the expense of state power, so long as it operates within the shadows of the omnipresent national power.

However, where the issue shifts from tribal independence from state power to the issue of tribal sovereignty over reservation populations, particularly non-members, the analysis takes on an entirely different dimension. In these cases, the Supreme Court's analysis reveals profound concerns about the operation of tribal power in the lives of US citizens who are not also members of the tribes. Tolerance for this deeper form of political autonomy would truly stretch the limits of legal pluralism, particularly since the constraints of the US Constitution do not apply against Indian tribes, as per the Court's holding in *Talton v. Mayes* (1896).[27] Vindicating tribal power in these circumstances would potentially touch sensitive and fundamental principles that go to the core of the nation's beliefs and values about legitimate government, individual rights, and the adhesive social contract that binds the two. The ideological challenge, in short, is determining precisely when we have reached the point of too much pluralism.

This was the challenge facing the Court in *Oliphant v. Suquamish Indian Tribe* (1978), where the issue was whether tribal inherent sovereignty could be exercised in a criminal prosecution against a white person who happened to be a reservation resident.[28] The Court ultimately held against tribal sovereignty in these circumstances. In subsequent chapters, we will examine the opinion and its progeny in considerably more detail. For now, it is important to point out that the Court's concerns about the constitutional values of liberty and due process were sufficient to allow it to act in a highly jurispathic way and kill off the juris-generative potential of tribal courts before they could do any serious damage to non-Indian American citizens. Before we leave the opinion, however, it may be helpful to consider the limited evidence we have of the in-chambers ruminations that took place about this case. From the papers of the late Thurgood Marshall comes a bench memorandum authored by the justice's law clerk, "vj," that contains a brief but sharp analysis of the legal issues in the case and an equivocal recommendation on how the justice should vote.[29] Despite the relative length of the piece, it is worth reproducing in its entirety:

> BENCH MEMO—Oliphant
> The question is whether Indian tribes, or this particular tribe, retain the sovereign right to try non-Indians for offenses occurring upon the reservation. The 1973 'law and order' code adopted by the Suquamish asserts jurisdiction over all types of offenses except those 'major crimes' defined in 18 U.S.C. 1153. Respt [Respondent] tribe asserts jurisdiction over neither Indians nor non-Indians charged with the 'major crimes.'
>
> The issue is very difficult, and I'm unable to form a strong or definite view. Starting from the premise that tribes do retain many attributes of internal sovereignty, however, it is clear that the right to try nonIndians for offenses committed on Indian territory (as these were) has never been expressly withdrawn from the tribes by general statute; and has not been withdrawn from this tribe by treaty. (Both treaties that the U.S. has with the Suquamish are silent on the question of the tribe's criminal jurisdiction.) It seems likely that Congress in the 19th century, in passing both the major crimes act and the General Crimes Act, 1152 probably assumed that tribes lacked jurisdiction over criminal offenses

committed by non-Indians; [inserted in hand-written script is the following clause] on a 'preemption' analysis, tribe may have lost their criminal jurisdiction. There is, however, some legislative histor [*sic*] going the other way; and in any event, such jurisdiction was never withdrawn.

I don't think the answer to this question will be found in legislative history, the statutes or the treaties. In my view, it comes down to balancing the real constitutional problems that will be created by holding that such jurisdiction exists, against the likely law enforcement problems that the tribes will have to endure if they are found not to possess criminal jurisdiction, at least over the relatively minor crimes at issue here which are unlikely to attract the interest of either state or federal prosecutors.

If non-Indians are held subject to Indian tribal court jurisdiction, the arguments in favor of holding the tribes to be 'federal instrumentalities' fully subject to the contraints [*sic*] on governmental power imposed by the Constitution will become much weightier; in light of the Indian Civil Rights Act of 1968, which extends all criminal procedure protection of the Bill of Rights (with the exception of the right to indictment by grand jury) to the tribes, this problem may not be as acute as it once was. On the other hand, if they are held not subject to tribal criminal jurisdiction, this holding might have the salutary effect of clarifying jurisdictional confusion which may have limited resource dedication to the problems of law enforcement on the reservation. However, such a ruling in favor of the petrs [petitioners] would also, at least in the near future, make tribal law enforcement very difficult, for reasons well set forth in several amici briefs: e.g., reservations are often far away from state centers of law enforcement; counties' unwillingness to committ [*sic*] resources to patrolling the reservation; absence of state laws which adequately protect Indian culture and attitude towards, e.g., graves and memorials. Since the Indian CRA [Civil Rights Act] also limits tribal courts in the amount of punishment that may be

> imposed (maximum is 6 months), the constitutional problems created by permitting tribal courts to try non-Indians are not as bad as they might otherwise be.
>
> If I had to make a recommendation, I would affirm CA9 [Court of Appeals for the Ninth Circuit] in holding that since Congress never took away tribe's criminal jurisdiction, they have it. But either view has support.
>
> vj[30]

Justice Marshall's law clerk proved prescient in suggesting that positive law would not likely provide the answer to the issues posed in the *Oliphant* case. The Court's majority opinion, authored by then Associate Justice William Rehnquist, acknowledged that the rule of decision in the case would come, not from treaties, statutes, or other expressions of congressional policy, but from the Court's views about the nature of the politico-legal relationship of dependency between tribes and the federal government. According to Justice Rehnquist, the treaties with the Suquamish by themselves,

> would probably not be sufficient to remove criminal jurisdiction over non-Indians if the Tribe otherwise retained such jurisdiction. But an examination of our earlier precedents satisfies us that, even ignoring treaty provisions and congressional policy, Indians do not have criminal jurisdiction over non-Indians absent affirmative delegation of such power by Congress. Indian tribes do retain elements of 'quasi-sovereign' authority after ceding their lands to the United States and announcing their dependency on the Federal Government. But the tribes' retained powers are not such that they are limited only by specific restrictions in treaties or congressional enactments. As the Court of Appeals recognized, Indian tribes are prohibited from exercising both those powers of autonomous states that are expressly terminated by Congress *and* those powers '*inconsistent with their status*'. (emphasis in original; citations omitted)[31]

As we will see shortly, the Court's understanding of "dependency" did not draw upon Chief Justice Marshall's notions of dependency as articulated in the *Cherokee Nation* cases, that were, in turn, derived from principles of international law. Instead, the *Oliphant* court looked to later nineteenth-century judicial precedents that stressed the tribes' "factual" dependency upon the federal government in terms of their daily subsistence and general well-being. In other words, the Court trained its jurisprudential eye on the historical period during which tribal sovereignty and political autonomy were under greatest assault by the United States through policies that devastated the tribal land base, brought thousands of homesteading non-Indians into Indian country as permanent residents, and severely crippled the self-governing capacities of tribes across the nation.

In similar fashion, the Court's modern-era Indian law jurisprudence has pointed to the expectations of non-Indian reservation residents (or occupants) as a critical element in locating the contours of inherent tribal power. The doctrinal relevance of examining such expectations becomes clear only if we see the exercise as part of the Court's effort to understand the national tolerance for such forms of legal pluralism and the degree to which our impulse toward national unity can accommodate deviations from the set of fundamental core principles, values, and norms that define the national societal and governance superstructure. One of the most explicit appeals to the expectations of non-Indian reservation residents appears in the Court's decision in *Montana v. United States* (1981).[32] In this case, the Court considered whether the scope of inherent tribal sovereignty included the power to apply tribal hunting and fishing regulations against non-Indian residents acting on lands they own in fee simple within the reservation. In finding against such tribal power, the Court extended the rule of *Oliphant* into the civil-regulatory realm and imposed yet another set of constraints on the exercise of tribal sovereign authority. We will consider the Court's analysis in more detail in a subsequent chapter but for present purposes, it is important to examine the Court's discussion of non-Indian expectations as to the reach of tribal law. Of particular significance (or concern) is the Court's focus on the expectations of citizens and policy makers from another historical era, the so-called Allotment era of the late nineteenth century, and whether those expectations could be or should be vindicated in the modern era. Here is what the Supreme Court had to say about these expectations:

> [N]othing in the Allotment Acts supports the view of the Court of Appeals that the Tribe could nevertheless bar hunting and fishing by non-resident fee owners. The policy of the Acts was the eventual assimilation of the Indian population, and the 'gradual extinction of Indian reservations and Indian titles.' The Secretary of the Interior and the Commissioner of Indian Affairs repeatedly emphasized that the allotment policy was designed to eventually eliminate tribal relations. And throughout the congressional debates on the subject of allotment, it was assumed that the 'civilization' of the Indian population was to be accomplished, in part, by the dissolution of tribal relations.
>
> There is simply no suggestion in the legislative history that Congress intended that the non-Indians who would settle upon alienated allotted lands would be subject to tribal regulatory authority. Indeed, throughout the congressional debates, allotment of Indian land was consistently equated with the dissolution of tribal affairs and jurisdiction. *It defies common sense to suppose that Congress would intend that non-Indians purchasing allotted lands would become subject to tribal jurisdiction when an avowed purpose of the allotment policy was the ultimate destruction of tribal government.* And it is hardly likely that Congress could have imagined that the purpose

> of peaceful assimilation could be advanced if feeholders could be excluded from fishing or hunting on their acquired property.
>
> The policy of allotment and sale of surplus reservation land was, of course, repudiated in 1934 by the Indian Reorganization Act. But what is relevant in this case is the effect of the land alienation occasioned by that policy on Indian treaty rights tied to Indian use and occupation of reservation land. (emphasis added)[33]

This catalogue of expectations is notable for its complete erasure of the expectations of tribal citizens. At the same time, the Court's approach places it in the curious and quite untenable position of completing the unfinished business of an earlier Congress—the ultimate destruction of tribal governments. The Court's reification of an explicitly repudiated congressional policy reveals the truth of James Madison's 1788 words to Thomas Jefferson that the danger of oppression comes from instances where the government operates as the mere instrument of the majority of the community. The Court's opinion manifests an utter lack of remorse or moral accountability for the federal policies that betrayed tribal expectations through undeserved violence and breach of treaty promises. To be clear, this is not to suggest that the Court ought to telescope present-day standards of morality to actors performing in an entirely different historical era in response to different circumstances. Rather, it is to indict the modern Court for its failure to account for the expectations of tribal citizens before settling upon a particularized narrative that would appease the majoritarian expectations for non-Indians living in Indian country. In this sense, William Connolly is exactly right that the "Indian is thus simultaneously the first Other of the civi-territorial complex, the first sign of violence inscribed in its boundaries, and the first marker of how violence is obscured or forgotten by the complex that requires it."[34]

What might such a more balanced accounting of expectations look like in a modern-day adjudicative setting? For an example, we might look to the opinion in *Confederated Salish & Kootenai Tribes of the Flathead Reservation v. Namen* (1982), decided by the Court of Appeals for the Ninth Circuit just a year after the Supreme Court's decision in *Montana.* In a dispute that upheld the tribe's rights to the portion of a lakebed lying within its reservation, the Court analyzed the expectations of Indian and non-Indian parties as follows:

> It may well be that non-Indians who acquired land inside the reservation never expected to be subjected to regulation by the Indians. But likewise the Indians themselves never expected, when the Hell Gate Treaty set aside the Flathead Reservation 'for the[ir] exclusive use and benefit' and barred non-Indians from living there without Indian assent, that reservation land opened without their consent to non-Indians would be removed from their jurisdiction. The Indians' expectations rest on the explicit guarantees of a treaty signed by the President and Secretary of State and ratified by the Senate. The non-Indians' expectations rest not on explicit statutory language, but on what is presumed to have been the intent underlying the allotment acts—a policy of destroying tribal government to assimilate the Indians into American society. It is difficult to see why there should be an overriding federal interest in vindicating only the latter expectations—especially when the anti-tribal policy on which they rest was repudiated over fifty years ago.[35]

The Ninth Circuit's analysis examines the underlying sources for the respective expectations to discern the moral strength of the claims in light of the certainty that one set of expectations would be rejected or at least forced to accommodate the other. In an important sense, the Court's analysis embraces Connelly's ethos of critical responsiveness by opening up "cultural space through which new possibilities of being might be enacted" and requiring adjustments or revisions among those whose hegemonic position depends, in part, upon maintaining comparative notions of social, cultural, and political superiority over others.[36] It is an analysis that redirects the national imaginary, however tentatively, in the direction of democratic pluralism, toward a discourse about intergovernmental relations that affirms the legitimacy and dignity of sovereign tribal governments within their territories. In short, the *Namen* court's analysis illustrates the potential for reviving our formative ethos of legal pluralism in the modern era by anchoring its legal narrative in a discourse that explicitly embraces, and indeed challenges, the moral integrity of the competing moral claims raised by Native and non-Native litigants.

CHAPTER 3

Pluralism and Liberalism: Testing the Limits of a Measured Separatism for Tribal Nations

The project of advancing tribal sovereignty in the United States through a revitalized ethos of legal pluralism encounters another, perhaps deeper, set of questions about the compatibility of pluralism and liberalism. The key concern here is whether a liberal democracy like the United States can, or should, accommodate the demands of Indian tribes for self-government. In accord with Will Kymlicka, liberalism here is taken to mean "a normative political philosophy, a set of moral arguments about the justification of political action and institutions."[1] With the *individual* as its bedrock moral unit, liberalism interrogates the legitimate reach of state action with the view toward maximizing individual freedom, autonomy, and equality.[2]

Liberalism's focus on individual freedom and equality has presented challenges for proponents of group rights, the broader category into which tribal sovereignty and rights of self-government are often cast. As Kymlicka has noted, "on the standard interpretation of liberalism, aboriginal rights are viewed as matters of discrimination and/or privilege, not of equality. They will always, therefore, be viewed with the kind of suspicion that [lead] liberals ... to advocate their abolition. Aboriginal rights, at least in their robust form, will only be secure when they are viewed, not as competing with liberalism, but as an essential component of liberal political practice."[3] The challenge for liberals, therefore, has been to locate a principled basis for supporting indigenous rights within the predominate political ideology of our time. This has required liberals, as a preliminary matter, to account for the pervasive social and cultural diversity or multicultural pluralism that exists in most societies, what some scholars call the "dilemma of difference."[4] Accounting for differences among the people may require the state to treat its citizenry on a differentiated basis (e.g., greater share of public resources or enhanced inclusion or participation and/or representation within the polity), a result in tension with, if not contrary to, liberalism's principle of equality.

To be sure, *illiberalism* exists to a certain degree in all societies, often with the tacit (or sometimes, express) support of the state. In other words, as Kymlicka notes, some cultures or groups "assign particular roles and duties to people, and prevent people from questioning or revising them."[5] Religious organizations, fraternal groups and orders, and other collectivities often contain strains of illiberalism as a component of their ideological and organizational structures. The Roman Catholic Church, for example, excludes women from ordination as members of the clergy; the Boy Scouts exclude openly gay individuals from leadership roles, both of which are protected illiberal practices under the Constitution.[6] In a broad sense, liberalism accommodates such practices under conditions where individuals within these collectivities are provided the opportunity to opt-out and to voice dissent against the illiberal practices. In the case of Indian tribes, the central question revolves around the degree of autonomy, or in Charles Wilkinson's phrase, *measured separatism*,[7] that Indian tribes can or should be accorded within a liberal democracy.

Scholars who see liberalism and pluralism as compatible argue from the basis of *value pluralism*, or in other words, the view that "multiple and incommensurable conceptions of the good [are] the starting point of liberalism."[8] From this perspective, individual freedom and autonomy are realized through the exercise of choice among diverse, competing (and sometimes conflicting) values that presupposes a diverse or plural society.[9] Moreover, since individual notions of identity are produced in association with others, typically within cultural groups, liberal pluralists maintain that the values of freedom and autonomy can extend to groups as well. In either case, the values of freedom and autonomy are contingent, not absolute, and must take into account the interests of others within the society. Diverse national minorities and indigenous peoples pose an additional challenge for the political community because their claims include demands for rights of self-government. In these instances, there is a risk of creating "illiberal pockets in plural societies." Scholars differ in their responses to these claims, with some expressing cautious support for multicultural pluralism operating within the orbit of state power and control, and others going further and demanding some accommodation on the part of the state itself, "even where there are internal practices many disagree with."[10]

Critics of the "compatibility thesis" argue that liberalism is simply "too individualist to fit in the group-centered world of pluralism." For these critics, the compatibility approach is "both too individualist in its focus—groups as the context for personal autonomy—and is in conflict with groups that simply may not value individual autonomy as much as liberals. Illiberal groups, especially, make pluralist/liberal compatibility tenuous, at best."[11]

Why are concerns about liberalism and its relation to pluralism relevant to this project? There are at least two significant reasons why proponents of tribal sovereignty should be mindful of these concerns. First, liberalism is the intellectual framework from which majoritarian policy makers, including judges, derive their understanding of rights and the limits of state power. Advancing claims for the protection of indigenous rights therefore has to proceed on terms that these policy makers will understand and respect.[12] Second, there is increasingly strong support for the view that the doctrinal confusion and incoherence that is rampant in federal Indian law is actually a symptom of deeper problems that reside closer to the subterranean levels of the American polity and implicate fundamental questions about the nature of sovereignty, plurinationalism, and the relationship between settler states and indigenous peoples. In 2004, Justice Clarence Thomas summarized the core problems in federal Indian law in these words:

> The Court should admit that it has failed in its quest to find a source of congressional power to adjust tribal sovereignty. Such an acknowledgment might allow the Court to ask the logically antecedent question *whether* Congress (as opposed to the President) has this power. A cogent answer would serve as the foundation for the analysis of the sovereignty issues posed by this case. We might find that the Federal Government cannot regulate the tribes through ordinary domestic legislation and simultaneously maintain that the tribes are sovereigns in any meaningful sense. But until we begin to analyze these questions honestly and rigorously, the confusion that I have identified will continue to haunt our cases. (emphasis in original)[13]

In light of these considerations, it is worth taking a closer look at how tribal claims to sovereignty and self-government can be accommodated within a liberal democracy like the

United States, an inquiry that will require us to consider the foundation upon which such tribal claims rest and even the appropriateness of articulating tribal political goals in the context of *sovereignty*. In framing the inquiry in this way, I am mindful of the positional deference I am according to the state. This is purposeful. The reason is because no credible tribal leader in the modern era articulates tribal sovereignty claims with the view toward displacing the state. Tribal leaders in the United States recognize, perhaps begrudgingly, that their aspirations to be self-determining nations will invariably take the form of limited powers of self-governance operating within the dominant polity. In similar fashion, the United Nations Declaration on the Rights of Indigenous Peoples recognizes a right of self-determination for indigenous peoples (Article 3) while explicitly preserving the territorial integrity and political unity of existing sovereign and independent states (Article 46). Thus, the inquiry that follows builds on the assumption that tribal governments seek to achieve meaningful forms of self-government in juridical spaces located within a host nation-state.

Arguments about the source and extent of an indigenous right to self-government vary widely. Margaret Moore offers one of the most thoughtful justifications to support an indigenous right to self-determination premised on liberal-democratic theories. Moore's analysis is anchored in the historical legacy of prior dispossession of indigenous lands and resources that is causally linked to present-day patterns of marginalization or disadvantage of indigenous people. In this setting, notions of *rectificatory justice* establish obligations on the part of the contemporary nonindigenous population, who have gained advantages and benefits from the acts of prior dispossession, to account for this state of affairs. While this argument supports limited differentiation among citizens in terms of the redistribution of goods (e.g., lands, resources, money) to indigenous peoples, it stops well short of restoring indigenous peoples to their original position. Such a result, Moore contends, would create new forms of injustice because "people build a pattern of expectations and attachment to land and goods that they are [now] in possession of."[14]

Moore's argument for rectificatory justice is supplemented by a liberal-democratic critique about the legitimacy of state power over indigenous peoples. This analysis builds upon contemporary liberal theory (as highlighted above) that recognizes the autonomy and freedom of groups to determine the optimal path to the good life and supports the group's claims for the resources and jurisdictional authority sufficient to realize their goals. In the context of indigenous groups, there is the added fact that the state often employed policies designed systematically to eradicate indigenous culture and identity. Moreover, their incorporation within the state typically proceeded upon nonconsensual terms and occurred within an atmosphere of coercion, duplicity, or fraud, especially in light of the state's failure to live up to treaty guarantees that purported to honor and protect the political and territorial integrity of Indian nations. Moore's analysis of the illegitimacy of state claims to wield power over indigenous peoples is worth reciting at length:

> An understanding of the bases of state legitimacy is important to the claims of indigenous peoples who implicitly question the authority of the state to govern them. In many cases, indigenous peoples were entirely excluded from the processes of state creation, which raises the question of the basis for the state's authority over indigenous peoples. If the exercise of legitimate authority is based on the principles of democratic consent and the sovereignty of the people, then the current state does not exercise legitimate authority over them. If indigenous peoples were entitled,

> through the same normative principle, to exercise collective self-government in the past, then how, normatively, has this right been extinguished? It is counterintuitive to suppose that the continued subordination and unfair treatment of indigenous peoples has left them also with fewer (moral) rights and no longer entitled to collective self-government.[15]

Moore's reliance on liberal-democratic theory has important implications for the nature and scope of indigenous self-government. First, she notes that since tribal self-government derives its force from the liberal interest in collective self-rule, their interests in advancing their cultural norms through democratic political means is an appropriate expression, though not a limitation, of their jurisdictional authority. In other words, Moore argues that indigenous peoples' rights to self-government are not *defined* by their distinct cultures or traditions. In her words, "the problem with traditional culture-based conceptions of indigenous peoples is that they tend to define indigenous people in purely traditional terms and indeed suggest that self-government should be conferred on indigenous people to the extent that they adhere to traditional ways and maintain their old culture. This fails to recognize the dynamic and adaptable nature of both culture and identity."[16] Anishinabe legal scholar John Borrows has called attention to this very problem in his critique of Canadian First Nation jurisprudence that interprets section 35(1) of the Constitution Act (1982). This provision states: "The existing Aboriginal and treaty rights of the Aboriginal peoples of Canada are hereby recognized and affirmed." Canadian courts interpret aboriginal rights to mean "those practices that were integral to the culture and traditions of Aboriginal peoples prior to the arrival of Europeans."[17] In this formulation, the scope of modern-day aboriginal rights is tied explicitly to an atavistic conception of indigenous cultural practices dating back to pre-European times. Indeed, Borrows suggests that section 35 "has not been sufficiently directed towards the larger project of [indigenous] nation-building" and, at a minimum, "should not be permitted to sidetrack all Canadians from the more fundamental work to be done to harmonize Indigenous peoples' relationships with their neighbours."[18]

Moore's second observation about the nature and scope of indigenous self-government is that it "should be consistent with the fundamental principles of democracy."[19] This conclusion leads her to question the application or relevance of territorial sovereignty in the case of indigenous peoples. The concept of *territorial sovereignty* traces back to the European Treaty of Westphalia in 1648, which signaled the end of the Christian church's moral and political hegemony and the rise of secular nation-states that exercised authority within a particular territory. The concept operates both to define the ultimate source of authority (i.e., the state) and the juridical space within which that authority is supreme. As one commentator has noted, "the acceptance of territorial sovereignty at the settlement of Westphalia brought to an end both imperial notions of authority and functionally defined claims to sovereignty, familiar from the 'two-sword theory' of medieval times. By assigning mutually exclusive areas for the exercise of this supreme authority, the sovereigns thenceforth accepted only this form of political organization as legitimate. They also found thereby a convenient way of squaring their claims to supremacy with the mutual recognition of equality. Sovereignty thus created both the territorial state and the international system."[20]

Moore's analysis here is quite significant because it touches on the subject that has most troubled the modern US Supreme Court, that is, the nature and scope of tribal sovereign authority over non-members of the tribe, especially nonindigenous people. Moore views territorial self-government as incompatible with political systems that are defined by and limited to members of a particular group or ethnic community. Territorial self-government, Moore argues,

> presupposes that all people resident within a particular jurisdiction, and so subject to its rules, have input or democratic voice in the making of these decisions. It is entirely legitimate to draw boundaries *around* areas of indigenous majorities and to ensure that the community has the jurisdictional authority to effectively control entry into the area (by regulating such things as housing permits) to prevent their local majority from being 'swamped' by a nonindigenous majority, if that is what they desire. However, it does not mean that they are entitled to disenfranchise nonindigenous people resident in their area or indeed to set rigid rules for membership that exclude or marginalize some people in the self-governing community. (emphasis in original)[21]

The modern US Supreme Court has embraced this aspect of Moore's liberal-democratic argument within its federal Indian common law jurisprudence and has relied, in part, on concepts of territoriality to impose severe limitations on the scope of inherent tribal powers. In *Duro v. Reina* (1990), the Supreme Court specifically referenced the concept of territorial sovereignty and found it inapplicable in the circumstances of Indian tribes: "A basic attribute of full territorial sovereignty is the power to enforce laws against all who come within the sovereign's territory, whether citizens or aliens. *Oliphant* [*v. Suquamish Indian Tribe*] recognized that the tribes can no longer be described as sovereigns in this sense. Rather, as our discussion in [*United States v.*] *Wheeler* reveals, the retained sovereignty of the tribes is that needed to control their own internal relations, and to preserve their own unique customs and social order."[22]

Thus, while Moore's liberal-democratic argument goes a long way in shoring up the arguments in favor of tribal self-government, it ultimately settles for a weak form of group self-government that operates internally within the tribal society. The argument does not address whether democratic principles should constrain the operation of tribal self-government in relation to its own membership, especially in light of the fact that tribal members are also citizens of the United States. Would or should such principles require, for example, that tribes whose traditional membership rules function along the lines of matrilineality or patrilineality reject such rules in favor of more egalitarian principles for group membership? If so, this would demonstrate that the structural imbalances of power in the state–indigenous relationship continue to constrain tribal self-government and force it to operate in a manner more consistent with, if not entirely identical to, the dictates of democratic normativity. In that instance, the state's political power would function as "the 'mere effect and continuation of a relation of domination' that is fundamental—'a perpetual relation of force'."[23]

Moore's critique also does not contemplate the possibility that the liberal-democratic interests of non-members of the tribe could be addressed or accommodated in other ways. It is quite conceivable that the state, on behalf of its non-member citizens, could negotiate with the tribes to produce a system of tribal self-governance that accords due weight and respect to the interests of the state's citizens. The Indian Civil Rights Act of 1968 (ICRA) actually represents one such example, although it hardly qualifies as a negotiated arrangement, since it was imposed by the US Congress upon tribes pursuant to the government's claimed plenary power in Indian affairs. The ICRA incorporates most, though not all, of the protections of the Bill of Rights and requires tribes to observe these rights in the exercise of their inherent sovereign powers.[24] In the *Oliphant* case, the Supreme Court noted that in "submitting to the overriding sovereignty of the United States, Indian tribes therefore necessarily give up their power to try nonIndian citizens of the United States *except in a manner acceptable to Congress*."[25] The Court later mentions the Indian Civil Rights Act but never addresses whether the Act represents Congress's prior acquiescence to tribal power over non-Indians acting within the tribe's territory.

Charles Wilkinson has suggested other strategies by which tribes seek to address and accommodate the interests of non-Indian citizens. While no tribe has apparently gone so far as to enfranchise non-Indian citizens in general tribal elections, many have created sub-tribal nation advisory boards on or through which non-Indian interests can be advanced.[26] There are also a wide range of intergovernmental agreements on water rights, criminal law enforcement, environmental protection and regulation, economic development, and taxation that embrace the interests of non-member residents of Indian country. These arrangements, often negotiated by the state or the federal governments in which all citizens are represented, including non-Indian citizens who reside in Indian country, would seem to advance liberal democracy's concerns for fairness and equality. In that context, it is worth noting that non-Indian citizens are actually members of the majoritarian society and in many reservations are also the majority population. The point here is that non-Indians, whatever their numerical reservation population, retain full access to the processes of the majoritarian state and thus have the opportunity to articulate their interests through the mechanism of those processes as it relates to living in Indian country.

In more recent years, Duncan Ivison has advanced an argument that, like Moore, conceives of liberalism as fully capable of supporting claims for indigenous self-determination but in forms that may extend beyond what Moore envisions. In his book, *Postcolonial Liberalism*, Ivison accepts the historical arguments of indigenous prior occupancy, their exercise of prior sovereignty and cultural continuity/persistence as vital and significant bases upon which to ground contemporary indigenous claims to self-determination (among other rights), but his argument in support of indigenous rights extends beyond these historical strands. Ivison identifies what he calls a *normative thesis* underlying aboriginal rights that justifies their claims "with reference not only to the self-understandings, laws, practices and particular historical circumstances of indigenous peoples, but also to more general principles of equality, freedom and well-being."[27] These principles, all bedrock values of classical liberalism, inform Ivison's view of the "postcolonial state" and the conditions that must exist in the political realm to mediate the interests of indigenous and nonindigenous peoples in ways that are acceptable to both. According to Ivison, "the main aim of the postcolonial state is to minimize domination, and pursuing equal recognition for indigenous peoples in the public sphere is a means to that end. But at the same time, the postcolonial state must ensure that its citizens, whatever their background, have the capacities to contest and modify the norms, practices, and rules that govern them."[28] The ideal embraced by postcolonial liberalism is what Ivison terms "*complex mutual coexistence*"[29] between indigenous and nonindigenous peoples, an aspirational goal that echoes, in significant ways, the normative philosophy underlying the Haudenosaunee's historic *Kaswentha*, or Two-Row Wampum. That formative instrument of indigenous intergovernmental diplomacy similarly embraced notions of mutual recognition, respect, and peaceful coexistence in shared territories.

To advance the aim of complex mutual coexistence, Ivison suggests that we focus less on securing access to the resources (e.g., rights and freedoms, income) that may be needed to secure the equality, freedom, and well-being of indigenous peoples (the *resourcist approach*) and place more attention on the *capabilities or functionings* that enable individuals to make meaningful and productive use of those resources (the *capabilities approach*). This approach builds on the conceptual work of the noted economist and philosopher Amartya Sen and draws attention to "real freedoms" that individuals can exercise as a matter of fact in order to achieve a state of well-being. The right to vote, for example, rings hollow if the individual has been deprived of a meaningful education that would enable informed participation in the electoral process, the means of transportation to reach election polls, or the means of communication to remain current on candidates and issues of the day. Ivison applies the capabilities approach to sketch the contours of the postcolonial state in these words:

> A postcolonial liberal order should aim to secure those capabilities required to participate effectively in collective practices of public reason that affect one's fundamental interests. What counts as a fundamental interest includes not only those very basic physiological and psychological needs that human beings everywhere share, but is also shaped by the particular forms of constructive social power—or constellation of discourses—circulating in the public sphere. The way capabilities are picked out and described is therefore crucial. Thus any proposed list or threshold of central capabilities has to be adequately deliberated and subject to contestation. That is, it has to emerge from a process in which the reasons that become authoritative in shaping governmental or social action in a particular domain can be shared by those subject to them. The focus then is not only on trying to identify those central capabilities that are required for being a 'normally cooperating member of society', but also the conditions under which agreements about these descriptions are said to be legitimacy-conferring.[30]

Ivison places important emphasis on both the substantive dimensions of the requisite capabilities and the procedural framework within which such capabilities are articulated, defended, and contested. Equally important, he calls attention to both internal and external factors that may impact upon the individual's choice or capability to act upon the resources available to them, as for example, the myriad social, economic, or cultural factors that may inhibit the effective delivery of health care in certain communities or pervasive social norms that effectively curb or constrain individual choice.

With the ideal of *complex mutual coexistence* in mind, Ivison contends that we ought to view indigenous rights, in their normative sense, as

> securing a particular kind of capability set in relation to Aboriginal peoples' interests in land, culture and self-government. These capabilities enable indigenous people to pursue their conceptions of the good and ways of life equally, since they promote a distribution of formal and constructive social power that takes into account the distinctive historical and social facts of their situation, both in the past and today. Securing Aboriginal peoples' interests to land recognizes their pre-existing territorial rights and protects their property interests, just as the law protects those of non-Aboriginal people. Securing their cultural interests enables Aboriginal peoples access to equal resources to maintain, adapt and reproduce their cultural identities, given the challenges they face in doing so. Securing their sovereign interests acknowledges Aboriginal nations as equal partners at the time of European contact, and contributes to their capacity to improve the substantive material and social inequalities their communities face today.[31]

Ivison's notion of complex mutual coexistence as the ideal of postcolonial liberalism anticipates that there will inevitably be clashes of norms and values between indigenous and nonindigenous normative orders, particularly as the interests of indigenous peoples become increasingly articulated and rendered functional in the broader society. In those instances of conflict, whose norms prevail and why, and by what mechanism are they resolved? Ivison offers three possible models for addressing these sorts of conflicts: (1) the *core–periphery approach*, which posits, in a priori fashion, a basic set of rights (or capabilities) that no normative order should violate or transgress; (2) the *deliberative approach*, which places a premium on the legitimating conditions within which individuals and groups assert and contest their claims; and (3) the *institutional design approach*, which envisions the creation of a framework for intersocietal and intergovernmental dialogue that avoids the accretion of political power in any one normative order in favor of a regime wherein power circulates among the respective authorities. In Ivison's terms, "instead of authority and jurisdiction always being a matter of belonging to either the state or the group, the institutional design approach accepts the multiplicity of possible jurisdictional lines and the need for coordination and interaction between them."[32] The model best suited to resolve an intersocietal or intergovernmental dispute would depend upon the nature of the conflicting interests. There may indeed be instances where the various approaches will overlap with and complement each other.

The force and utility of Ivison's notion of postcolonial liberalism and its attendant ideal of complex mutual coexistence is most glaringly apparent in the context of assessing tribal authority over non-members of indigenous communities, the issue that has most troubled the modern Supreme Court. Unlike Moore, whose understanding of territorial sovereignty leads her, like the Supreme Court, to place severe limits on the power of Indian tribes to reach non-members, Ivison rightly draws our attention to the interstices of intergovernmental relations, the juridical space "in between" indigenous and nonindigenous polities where values and norms can be articulated and contested in an ongoing dialogic fashion and where institutional arrangements of various kinds can be developed to give expression to and protection for the resulting mediated set of values and norms. Within this framework, there are no presuppositions about the precedence or primacy to be accorded to competing jurisdictions, in part because there is an understanding that group members may share overlapping interests and affinity with the values and norms of their fellow citizens in the broader society.

To illustrate the intrinsic value of Ivison's approach, let us consider the protection of individual liberty, the constitutional value of greatest concern to the Supreme Court in *Oliphant v. Suquamish Indian Tribe*. In its opinion, the Court noted, "from the formation of the Union and the adoption of the Bill of Rights, the United States has manifested an equally great solicitude that its citizens be protected by the United States from unwarranted intrusions on their personal liberty."[33] The Court of Appeals for the Ninth Circuit, which upheld the tribe's inherent criminal jurisdiction over non-Indians like Oliphant, was equally mindful of the liberty interest but concluded that the protections afforded by the Indian Civil Rights Act were sufficient to safeguard Oliphant's interests in tribal court. The appeals court also noted that ICRA includes what Ivison calls a "reversal point"—the writ of habeas corpus—to challenge the legality of tribal court proceedings in federal court. Importantly, the appeals court noted that tribal criminal jurisdiction over non-Indians advanced the federal policy of encouraging the development of tribal institutions of self-government; "[t]ribal criminal jurisdiction over non-Indians, as limited by the Indian Bill of Rights, is a small but necessary part of this policy."[34] Moreover, the appeals court recognized that tribal jurisdiction over non-Indians advanced the very practical objectives of law enforcement in Indian communities, particularly for minor offenses that rarely attract the attention or priority of federal (or in certain circumstances, state) officials. This conclusion helped secure the tribal community's interest in public safety and community cohesion and indeed, its interest in the integrity of its governmental institutions. In the words of the appeals court, "Public safety is an underpinning of a political entity. If tribal members cannot protect themselves from offenders, there will be powerful motivation for such tribal members to leave the Reservation, thereby counteracting the express Congressional policy of improving the quality of Reservation life.... The dignity of the tribal government suffers in the eyes of Indian and non-Indian alike, and a tendency toward lawless behavior necessarily follows."[35]

There are elements of both the *core–periphery* and the *institutional design* approaches at work in the appeals court's analysis. Two sets of interests (or capabilities)—an individual interest in personal liberty and a collective interest in public safety—are identified as threshold elements that must exist in civil society to promote individual and group well-being. The Indian Civil Rights Act functions as the mechanism of institutional design through which jurisdictional power flows in order to vindicate these competing interests, beginning initially in the tribal courts, and in the event of perceived failures there, in the federal courts. The appeals court's analysis (unlike that of the Supreme Court) eschews any presuppositions about the justice-rendering capacities of the tribal courts and instead accepts, consistent with the institutional design approach, the "multiplicity of possible jurisdictional lines and the need for coordination and interaction between them."[36] By securing an important measure of "on the ground" sovereign authority, an orientation toward the "local" in Ivison's formulation, the appeals court in *Oliphant* furthered the tribal community's interest in public safety and enhanced the legitimacy of their tribal institutions by recognizing them as capable of rendering justice to all persons—Indian and non-Indian alike—who stand trial in tribal courts.

Arguably, the appeals court resolution of the jurisdictional issue in *Oliphant* fulfills Ivison's injunction for postcolonial liberalism which "aims for a state of affairs in which the legitimacy of the norms, practices and institutions upon which people's well-being depends inheres in a form of social and political conversation—or embodied argument—about what is legitimate and illegitimate; an argument that is ultimately 'without any guarantor and without any end'."[37] In other words, the appeals court situated the tribal courts as being in a dynamic conversation with their federal counterparts on the subject of individual liberty, with a focus on how best to protect it while also securing the tribe's interests in public safety and self-government. Unfortunately, on appeal to the US Supreme Court, the *Oliphant* majority short-circuited that intergovernmental conversation by reifying the colonialist-era positioning of tribes as inferior subnational entities and reverting to negative presuppositions about the justice-rendering capacities of tribal courts.

To be sure, the presence of an explicit "reversal point" in the Indian Civil Rights Act undoubtedly influenced the appeals court to take a more solicitous view of tribal courts, at least in cases where individual liberty is at issue. Where personal liberty is not at issue, however, the writ of habeas corpus allowing entry into federal court is unavailable to individuals seeking relief from tribal court authority. In those circumstances, the necessity of providing reversal points becomes much more complicated. From Ivison, we know that the preference is for a *negotiated*, rather than an *imposed*, set of options and alternative fora acceptable to both the indigenous and nonindigenous polities, to avoid the taint of illegitimacy or coercion. This outcome is a function of the *deliberative approach*, which posits the following: "any rules or norms of recognition and distribution proposed must be discursively legitimated, which in turn means that the conditions for reasonable deliberation be secured both within and between the state and the group."[38]

The intergovernmental arrangements suggested by Ivison would thus seem to accord with principles of *deliberative democracy*, a normative principle that assesses the legitimacy of law based, in part, on the nature of participation by those constituents potentially affected by the law and on notions of institutional transparency and accountability. Like Ivison, Steven Wheatley places a high premium on the deliberative process in his treatment of indigenous rights and their claims to self-government. Building on the work of Jürgen Habermas, Wheatley accepts the premise that indigenous legal systems and laws ought to reflect democratic principles if they are to apply within liberal states. On the issue of consent, however, Wheatley suggests that the demands of deliberative democracy do not require actual consent of the affected constituents so long as the laws in question are "cleansed of any odour of coercion."[39] The key is for citizens to view the resulting law as the product of their collective self-determination, either through their individual efforts or those of representatives acting through institutional processes endorsed by the citizens.[40] As noted earlier, many, if not most, of the intergovernmental arrangements operating in tribal communities today would appear to meet that threshold.

Closely aligned with Ivison, but writing more directly from the perspective of legal pluralism and the situation of First Nations in Canada, Tim Schouls offers further support for the principle of tribal self-government that also extends beyond the normative limits suggested earlier by Moore.

Schouls anchors his argument in favor of tribal self-government in the context of what he calls *relational pluralism*, one of the three faces of pluralism (along with *communitarian* and *individualist* pluralism). By way of background, Schouls understands pluralism as a "political principle that requires the state to act in ways to protect group diversity by not discriminating against social groups and, more positively, by acting in the domain of public policy to ensure their ongoing viability. These are commonly referred to as pluralist accommodations."[41] The communitarian and individualist faces of pluralism, according to Schouls, rely heavily on the identification and maintenance of group cultural differences, a factor that limits their effectiveness as an argument in support of tribal self-government. He notes, along with Ivison, that Will Kymlicka supports indigenous rights as a form of minority rights to a distinct culture. According to Kymlicka, it is through membership in these distinct cultural groups that the individual derives his or her sense of what is truly meaningful in life. The demands of liberalism thus require the state to act in ways that preserve these distinct cultural structures, or in Kymlicka's terms, "context of choice," so that the individual can make meaningful decisions about their lives.[42]

Relational pluralism, on the other hand, places less stock on distinct cultural differences and more on "subjective self-identification, relationships, and the formative role that power has in shaping individual and communal identity."[43] Schouls provides the following summary of relational pluralism that is worth recalling in some detail:

> [In the context of relational pluralism] there is no requirement that pluralism needs to be both defined and measured by the degree

> to which groups are culturally, politically, or socially different from one another. This point bears reinforcing. Instead, group difference is established as a function of relations; it exists in places where relations among people result in choices being made about establishing boundaries between people so that certain ties of group identification can be nurtured (e.g. ancestry) and objectives fulfilled (e.g. community development). What boundaries do is relate two or more distinct groups of people together who, despite sharing some or perhaps many cultural and political attributes, nevertheless find it important to remain distinct. Relational pluralism accentuates the idea that, in the exercise of drawing boundaries, those who relate across them are not necessarily concerned about preserving unique cultural and/or political content. Instead, what they seek to do is establish a relationship in which the members of distinct communities accept that neither side will invade or attempt to dominate the other as each pursues its respective self-defining processes. What makes this form of pluralism 'relational' is the fact that the degree of separation between groups is the product of an agreement secured between them; it can be greater or lesser depending on the respective aspirations of the group members involved.[44]

According to Schouls, approaching indigenous–state relations from the perspective of relational pluralism allows us to focus appropriately on the actual state of relations between the two polities. The institutional mechanisms designed to facilitate these intersocietal and intergovernmental relations are important, but Schouls views them as secondary from the standpoint of justice. For Schouls, "[w]hat is paramount are the actual relationships between Aboriginal and [state] governments; they should be built on duties of internal noninterference and commitments to equality in areas of mutually agreed on external interdependence. Put differently, where understandings negotiated between Aboriginal governments and the [state] are based on the full participation and consent of both parties, we can say that the Aboriginal right to self-government is being realized."[45]

As noted above, relational pluralism is centrally concerned with the formative role that power plays in shaping identity (both individual and community) and in shaping intergovernmental relations. Schouls concludes his analysis of relational pluralism by highlighting its utility as a normative theory:

> As a normative theory, relational pluralism shifts the object of our reflection about self-government to the more complex and ubiquitous question of Aboriginal community power. For relational pluralists, one judges the justice of the [state's] political system in part by the degree of independence and self-direction permitted to Aboriginal governments in their relations with the [state]. The standard of justice in this scheme is relational rather than cultural. Here real pluralism is marked by the capacity of the [state] to leave Aboriginal communities the power to change and grow on their own terms, free of [state] governmental domination. Naturally, what Aboriginal communities require to be free of domination will vary depending on the priorities that each community sets for its own jurisdictional independence. More broadly, however, the essential point that relational pluralists make is that Aboriginal self-government is justified not because it protects an Aboriginal right to cultural difference but because it promotes the Aboriginal right to use community resources of ancestry, history shared commitment, culture, land, and politics to build communities that correspond to their own priorities, whether culturally distinct or otherwise.[46]

With this extended background of Schouls's understanding of relational pluralism, we can return to his views on the source of the aboriginal right to self-government. Like Moore, Schouls grounds this right in a historical context but with a focus, not on prior dispossession, but on the formative relations that defined the reciprocal set of obligations undertaken by the colonial and aboriginal governments. This is akin to my earlier suggestion that formative US–tribal political relations reflected an ethos of legal pluralism. Schouls identifies two particular aspects of the relational history that are significant to the right of aboriginal self-government: the fact of *original occupancy* and the persistence of *community*. For Schouls, aboriginal self-government "originates from an Aboriginal status as organized political communities, rooted in territory, with an independent existence prior to the creation of the new state now called Canada." In addition, aboriginal self-government "is activated by the collective Aboriginal desire to have the political, social, and economic instruments to guarantee the development of their communities."[47]

Schouls's analysis leads him to suggest that contemporary forms of federalism are best suited to advance the mutual interests of aboriginal peoples and the state. The formal acts by which these interests are advanced need not necessarily take the form of treaties. For Schouls, the important point from the perspective of relational pluralism is that the formal acts embody genuine agreement on issues of shared concern produced in a setting of freedom, respect, and meaningful dialogue. One can easily see the normative parallels to Ivison's deliberative and institutional design approaches to achieving the state of complex mutual coexistence.

There are several highly appealing aspects of Schouls's relational pluralism argument in support of tribal self-government within liberal states. First, his emphasis on *subjective self-identification* seems to respond well to a general criticism of legal pluralist thought offered by Martha-Marie Kleinhans and Roderick MacDonald. These scholars suggest that legal pluralism tends to focus on the *real sites of law*, or in other words, the various spaces, communities, or locales within which law is produced and implemented. This focus often leads legal pluralists to ask questions about which legal order has primacy over others in a particular circumstance. This inquiry, however, tends to ignore the *subjects* of such legal orders and their perspectives on which legal order they identify with or belong to. The question posed by *critical* legal pluralism, according to Kleinhans and MacDonald, is this: "Within which legal order does the particular legal subject perceive himself or herself to be acting—whether resisting or sustaining?"[48] This inquiry places the spotlight on the citizen-subject and views them as sources of normativity in the sense that they are *law inventing*, not merely *law abiding,* forces within a society. A critical legal pluralism would thus go further in exposing and giving voice to substate societies whose demands for group recognition and respect are often drowned out by the homogenizing forces of the liberal state. In the process, it would also challenge the assumed neutrality of the liberal democratic state in relation to culture and society. Stephen Tierney has argued for just such a challenge in his analysis of national pluralism and constitutional law. For Tierney, the problem lies in liberalism's blind spot about the fact of social and cultural pluralism, or the state of plurinationalism within the nation-state. Liberalism's prescriptions about fairness, equality, and justice, according to Tierney, presume—incorrectly—the existence of a "unified *demos*." Our persistent failure to address the plurinational realities of the state risks the continued subordination of substate societies and the violation of the very principles advanced by liberalism. A key element to addressing this problem, says Tierney, is to focus more attention on the individual citizen's sense of identity and loyalty vis-à-vis the state and his/her substate society. "For the liberal nationalist," Tierney argues, "these variegated identity and loyalty patterns have important implications for the citizen as political and constitutional participant, since only by the proper recognition of the sub-state national society as a full and equal partner in the state can individual members of such a society find themselves able to play a full part in the plurinational polity."[49] Tierney's analysis is thus in line with Schouls's notion of subjective self-identification and the mode of inquiry suggested by Kleinhans and MacDonald.

Schouls's notion of relational pluralism, with its emphasis on subjective self-identification, is important in one other respect. It provides a principled means of accounting for, and assessing state obligations to, the significant population of American Indians living in urban areas. According to the 2000 Census, approximately two-thirds of the national American Indian population live outside of Indian country, the vast majority living in urban areas.[50] The urbanization of the American Indian population became a staple of federal Indian policy in the post–World War II era through the government's Indian relocation program. Federal agencies provided various forms of support to aid reservation Indians in their transition to city life. Urbanization in the late twentieth century played much the same role as agrarianism in the late nineteenth century in terms of facilitating the federal project of assimilating Indian people into the social and political life of the nation-state.[51] Schouls's notion of relational pluralism takes account of both the subjective self-identification of displaced Indian persons as members of their respective tribal nations, as well as the asymmetrical power arrangements that led to their relocation into urban centers. From the perspective of liberal democracy, federal expenditures in favor of urban Indians are justified as a continuation of the indigenous–state relations and obligations that may flow from treaties or their equivalent arrangements. Indeed, Congress acknowledges its obligations to provide health care to urban Indians in light of the federal government's causal role in the process of Indian urbanization.[52]

Finally, Schouls's notion of relational pluralism is appealing for its key focus on the normative assertions of power in the indigenous–state relationship. Building on the social reality that most individual Indian citizens occupy and contribute to multiple legal orders (i.e., their own tribal nations and the nation-state), this aspect of relational pluralism allows us to interrogate whether individuals are able to negotiate across social, cultural, and political boundaries in a manner that is free of interference, domination, or coercion (overt or systemic). In its communal form, this expression of indigenous self-identity serves as the foundation for the indigenous right of self-determination. The intergovernmental arrangements between the state and the indigenous governments can thus be assessed in light of their capacity to advance this core expression of indigenous self-identity. To the extent that these arrangements are also free of interference, domination, or coercion (overt or systemic), they will reflect what I have termed the formative ethos of legal pluralism in indigenous–state relations.

Beyond the arguments raised by Moore, Ivison, and Schouls (among others), liberal pluralists have advanced a further rationale for supporting the self-government claims of indigenous peoples. In essence, the claim suggests that the liberal state may derive benefits from actions that secure the political and territorial integrity of indigenous peoples. The benefits operate in related but distinct ways. First, the integrity and stability of the liberal state may be enhanced through measures that promote indigenous self-identification at both the individual and communitarian levels. State measures that go in the opposite direction and seek to impose a common citizenship upon indigenous peoples have typically failed, largely because they are perceived by indigenous peoples as (in)direct assaults on their existence as a people. Further, such culturally and politically homogenizing measures may serve as catalysts for internecine conflicts that can lead to further marginalization and oppression or even demands for secession. Will Kymlicka, one of the proponents of these views, calls attention to studies that show ethnonationalist conflicts escalate in states that reject or abandon self-government arrangements for national minorities and indigenous peoples, while they diminish in those states that are accommodating to such arrangements. In short, Kymlicka maintains, "if there is a viable way to promote a sense of solidarity and common purpose in a multination state, it will involve accommodating, rather than subordinating, national identities. People from different national groups will only share an allegiance to the larger polity if they see it as the context within which their national identity is nurtured, rather than subordinated."[53]

The second prong of this benefits thesis is the idea that indigenous societies have much to contribute to the dominant society in terms of normative political, cultural, and social values and knowledge about institution building. Burke Hendrix has distilled some of the major points of conceptual difference between indigenous and nonindigenous (or Western) society and offers this perspective: "The first and most overtly political is a commitment to a noncoercive kind of political life; the second and somewhat more diffuse politically is a focus on the value of community and the importance of relationships rather than rights; the third and most theological involves the place of humans in the larger order of the world and universe."[54]

While each of these points of conceptual difference between indigenous and Western perspectives is quite valid, for our purposes, it is Hendrix's first point of conceptual difference that I find particularly salient and worth closer inspection. To illustrate the point about indigenous commitment to noncoercive forms of political life, Hendrix refers to the work of Taiaiake Alfred. In addition to lending support to the proposition Hendrix advances, it is important to note that Alfred also takes serious issue with the indigenous political strategy of framing their political goals and objectives in the context of *sovereignty*. For Alfred, this involves invoking statist conceptions of political organization and practice that is problematic in at least two ways. First, it represents a significant move away from traditional indigenous forms of self-governance that are defined by consensus, nonhierarchical structures, and the absence of coercion. Second, it represents a capitulation to the nation-state's dominance and reinscribes the powers of the state over indigenous people that are deeply flawed and illegitimate.[55] Alfred's preference is to proceed with a discourse of indigenous nationhood but as Dale Turner points out, this, too is a normative discourse that is heavily freighted with Western conceptions of political power.[56] Like Schouls, Turner places more stock on the nature and quality of the politico-legal arrangements between indigenous peoples and the state and seeks to interrogate the context in which those arrangements were negotiated to determine their viability in a moral sense.

The preceding analysis has attempted to highlight some of the conceptual challenges policy makers and jurists face in attempting to accommodate tribal rights to self-government within the liberal state. The careful work of scholars like Moore, Ivison, and Schouls, among others, suggests that liberalism is capable of embracing the interests of tribal governments and their claims to self-determination. Indian tribal leaders are equally, if not more, cognizant of the imperatives of liberalism as they relate to the operation of their legal systems. Frank Pommersheim, a leading scholar of federal Indian law and Supreme Court justice for two Lakota tribes in South Dakota, has written eloquently about the role that tribal courts play in mediating the external normative demands of the nation-state (the demands "from above") while being faithful and responsive to values, norms, and traditions of their primary constituents, the tribal community (demands "from below"). For Pommersheim, tribal courts are the *crucibles of sovereignty* and represent the best assurance against federal intervention or encroachment in this sense: "[I]t is the wisdom and integrity of tribal law and tribal courts, properly and consistently informed by tradition and evolving contemporary tribal standards, that will stand as the best bulwark against federal encroachment. Without this continuing development, there can be little expectation for stability and equilibrium."[57] Tribal jurists and policy makers therefore need no reminders about the Supreme Court's admonition in *Oliphant v. Suquamish Indian Tribe* (1978), that the exercise of tribal powers "is constrained so as not to conflict with the interests of [our] overriding sovereignty."[58]

In bringing this portion of the analysis to a close, it may be fitting to consider once more the relationship between tribal sovereign power and tribal rights of self-determination. Following Allen Buchanan, I accept his understanding of self-determination as a value or an interest having high moral significance that may be served by various degrees or forms of political autonomy, including, in its most robust form, sovereignty.[59] Although the term *sovereignty* has undergone considerable revision in recent years by scholars from various disciplines, it continues to stand for many people as a form of supreme and independent authority. Whether Indian tribes can or should articulate their political goals in the language of sovereignty is highly contested, as shown above. Conceptually, such strategies confound the traditional understanding of sovereignty because they conjure the notion of an *imperium in imperio*, a sovereign within a sovereign (or dominium within dominium). And yet, the actual state of relations between Indian tribes and the United States in the formative years envisioned precisely this sort of arrangement, with the understanding that tribes possessed and exercised inherent, not delegated, authority as an expression of collective self-determination. Interestingly, this mirrors the historical development of the concept of sovereignty itself. Robert Jackson notes that sovereignty was not "originally or primarily an abstract idea fashioned by philosophers and other theoreticians and then applied in practice. It is an expedient idea worked out by kings and other rulers, and their representatives and agents, in response to the novel circumstances of sixteenth- and seventeenth-century Europe. *The political arrangements and legal practices of sovereignty came first, the academic theories later.*" (emphasis added).[60] Over the years, the realities of the tribal–federal relationship have dramatically tilted the balance of power heavily in favor of the federal government and contributed to the steady suppression of both the practical and conceptual expressions of the formative notions of tribal sovereignty. Still, the conception of tribes as sovereign bodies with inherent powers of self-government was entrenched early on in American law and continues to operate in federal Indian law today, a fact that both complicates our modern-day efforts to understand the place of Indian tribes within our constitutional democracy and compels us to be mindful of tribal expectations regarding their self-governing aspirations that are rooted in those formative arrangements.

CHAPTER 4

Of Guardian and Wards: The Indian as *Homo Sacer*

The late anthropologist and writer Michael Dorris (Modoc) once observed, "Indian peoples were perceived not as they were but as they *had* to be, from a European point of view" (emphasis in original).[1] In the context of contemporary federal Indian law, one finds ubiquitous references to tribes and Native peoples as "peculiar" and "anomalous," in addition to earlier references as "strange," "savage," "helpless," and "uninformed." This *peculiarization* of Native peoples by federal policy makers was a necessary rhetorical and ideological move in America's nation-building project.[2] Aside from the ever-present specter of latent (or blatant) racism, the necessity to treat Native peoples as *Other* arose, in large part, from the founders' creation of a republican form of government that emphasized the qualities of social cohesion and cultural homogeneity. As historian Gordon S. Wood observed, the founders were keenly aware that monarchies and republics were "designed for very different societies":

> Republicanism put a premium on the homogeneity and cohesiveness of its society. By contrast, monarchies could comprehend large territories and composite kingdoms and peoples with diverse interests and ethnicities. Monarchies had their unitary authority, kingly honors and patronage, hereditary aristocracies, established national churches, and standing armies to hold their diverse societies together. Republics had none of these adhesive elements. Instead, republics were supposed to rely for cohesion on the moral qualities of their people—their virtue and their natural sociability. Monarchy imagined its society in traditional and prenational terms, as a mosaic of quasicorporate communities, and thus had little trouble in embracing African slaves and Indians as subjects. But republicanism created citizens, and since citizens were all equal to one another, it was difficult for the Revolutionaries to include blacks and Indians as citizens in the new republican states they were trying to create. This emphasis on republican homogeneity and equal citizenship meant that republics, as Montesquieu had indicated, should be small in size.[3]

The vast cultural diversity existing even at the founding of America, coupled with the conventional wisdom about the social and cultural homogeneity of republics, required the founders to "stretch the truth in emphasizing that Americans were actually one people with one destiny."[4] According to Wood, the social adhesive for the emerging American state was not a common nationality but a commitment to a common ideology, a belief in the liberal democratic principles of liberty, equality, and freedom. Whereas, European states typically emerged from pre-state nationalities forming new political structures, the American experience operated in reverse: "We Americans created a state before we were a nation, and much of our history has been an effort to define the nature of that nationality."[5]

The process of constructing a national imaginary included pushing out, marginalizing, and/or assimilating those diverse cultural and social elements that defied the ethos of republican cultural homogeneity. It is in this context that we can understand the early and persistent peculiarization of American Indians in the emerging narratives of law and federal Indian policy. The focus of this chapter is to examine how this strategy of peculiarization morphed from an ideological conceit designed to create distance between Indian people and citizens of the new republic into an instrumentality of law that became the underpinning for a radicalized plenary federal power that allowed the national government to empire at will over tribal nations and Indian people. In particular, we will examine how the meaning of concepts like *incorporation* and *dependency* evolved over the years and functioned to inhibit, if not totally suppress, the formative ethos of legal pluralism that characterized the state of indigenous-federal relations in the early years of the republic. In this effort, we will have occasion to consider the work of Italian philosopher Giorgio Agamben and his revival of the ancient Roman designation of *homo sacer* or "sacred man" through which he examines the exercise of exceptional sovereign power over an increasingly powerless subject, one denuded of virtually all political rights and exposed to sovereign law as a "bare life."

"UPON INCORPORATION": THE INDIAN AS "INSIDER" OUTSIDER

As noted earlier, the Supreme Court's decision in *Oliphant v. Suquamish Indian Tribe* (1978) held that the inherent sovereign authority of Indian tribes did not encompass the power to prosecute non-Indian offenders. The core of the Court's reasoning is embraced in the following passages:

> Indian tribes do retain elements of 'quasi-sovereign' authority after ceding their lands to the United States and announcing their

dependence on the Federal Government. But the tribes' retained powers are not such that they are limited only by specific restrictions in treaties or congressional enactments. As the Court of Appeals recognized, Indian tribes are prohibited from exercising both those powers of autonomous states that are expressly terminated by Congress *and* those powers '*inconsistent with their status*.' (emphasis in original)

Indian reservations are 'a part of the territory of the United States.' Indian tribes 'hold and occupy [the reservations] with the assent of the United States, and under their authority.' Upon incorporation into the territory of the United States, the Indian tribes thereby come under the territorial sovereignty of the United States and their exercise of separate power is constrained so as not to conflict with the interests of this overriding sovereignty. '[T[heir rights to complete sovereignty, as independent nations, [are] necessarily diminished.' (citations omitted)[6]

The Court goes on to discuss what were then understood to be the only two implied limitations upon inherent tribal sovereignty recognized in federal Indian law that resulted from the tribes' incorporation into the United States—the tribal power freely to transact for their lands and the power to engage in foreign relations. These limitations were necessitated, according to the Court, to advance the sovereign's interest in protecting its territory from internal diminishment and external threats. In *Oliphant*, the Court added a third implied limitation—the power to prosecute non-Indians—that was necessitated to vindicate the sovereign's interest in ensuring that the personal liberty of its citizens would be protected "from unwarranted intrusions."

The Court does not define what it means by "incorporation" nor does it provide any contextual information to explain in what sense and at what time tribes were so incorporated. At least one commentator has expressed doubt that any such evidence could be produced; he called the Court's invocation of incorporation a "performative utterance."[7] Furthermore, the Court's reference to tribes "announcing their dependence" upon the federal government suggests that tribes freely negotiated for and consented to their subordinated status. Indeed, the passage above imposes an ahistorical consentience upon an entire course of historical relations between tribes and the national government and the resulting political arrangements that emerged between the two polities. Those relations and resulting arrangements were marked, if anything, by bitter contestation over lands and peoples, substantial ideological disagreement on forms and exercise of political power, and struggles over efforts to align largely incommensurable values regarding justice, power, and equality.

On the other hand, the Court may have opted to remain purposefully vague about the meaning of incorporation, especially given its multivalent meanings in law and in political history and theory. While there is no credible evidence to support that view, there may be value nonetheless in exploring the multiple meanings of incorporation in the domains of law and political history and theory to see if indeed the concept works in the direction of further subordination of Indian tribes to the national power (as suggested in *Oliphant*) or whether it offers the potential for tribes to realize a greater measure of political autonomy as self-governing nations.

Incorporation in the Domain of Federal Indian Law

The Supreme Court has employed the notion of incorporation in at least two areas of US jurisprudence, in its federal Indian law cases and in cases dealing with newly acquired territories, particularly those lying outside the contiguous boundaries of the continental United States. In these areas of law, incorporation seems to function both to prescribe the nature of rights possessed by the denizens of the newly acquired territories and to chart the limits of federal power to manage or otherwise govern those territories. We will examine the Court's use of the incorporation doctrine beginning with its federal Indian law cases. As we will see, by the end of the nineteenth century, the Court's federal Indian law and federal territorial law cases were employing the concept of incorporation to support American imperialism abroad and at home. In fact, the doctrine played a critical role in supporting the nation's ruthless domestic campaign to eradicate all traces of indigeneity in the country by way of a judicially created federal plenary power in Indian affairs.

In the first federal Indian law case to employ the concept of incorporation, *Johnson v. M'Intosh* (1823), the Court effectively made Indian tribes guests in their own homelands by holding that the international law-derived doctrine of discovery placed ultimate title to their lands in the hands of the discovering Christian colonizing nation.[8] Tribes were left with a residual property interest denominated a *right of occupancy* that was subordinated only to the interests of the national sovereign. The sovereign's title by virtue of discovery gave it the exclusive right to "extinguish the Indian title of occupancy, either by purchase or by conquest; and gave also a right to such a degree of sovereignty, as the circumstances of the people would allow them to exercise."[9] According to the Court, title derived by conquest is acquired and maintained by force, but is tempered by humanitarian concerns to preserve the conquered as far as practicable. "Most usually," said the Court, "[the conquered] are incorporated with the victorious nation, and become subjects or citizens of the government with which they are connected. The new and old members of the society mingle with each other; the distinction between them is gradually lost, and they make one people. Where this incorporation is practicable, humanity demands, and a wise policy requires, that the rights of the conquered to property should remain unimpaired; that the new subjects should be governed as equitably as the old, and that confidence in their security should gradually banish their painful sense of being separated from their ancient connexions, and united by force to strangers."[10]

The discovery doctrine brought tribal lands under the ownership of the discovering sovereign nation, subject to the Indians' right of occupancy, and produced what Alex Tallchief Skibine has called the *geographical incorporation* of the tribal estate.[11] However, the Court's opinion makes clear that Indian tribes were not subjected to what we might call *political incorporation.* In other words, while the tribes' political status was subordinated to that of the discovering sovereign, their political autonomy was preserved, subject to the implied constraints noted above that were presumed to be the inevitable collateral damage of the colonial project. Their status as "fierce savages," a "people with whom it was impossible to mix," rendered the normative rules between conquerors and conquered inapplicable and required the application of new rules "better adapted to the actual state of things." Indeed, the only sociopolitical incorporation the *Johnson* court envisioned was in the case of a non-member of the tribe who voluntarily aligned himself/herself with a tribe and acquired lands under their laws. According to the Court, "[t]he person who purchases lands from the Indians, within their territory, incorporates himself with them, so far as respects the property purchased; holds their title under their protection, and subject to their laws. If they annul the grant, we know of no tribunal which can revise and set aside the proceeding."[12] This reveals an important truth about the *Johnson* case that is often overlooked or mischaracterized in the legal discourse. Properly understood, *Johnson* recognized a restraint on *purchase,* not a restraint on *alienation*, of Indian lands, limiting the universe of purchasers of Indian lands to the United States and those who acted with the imprimatur of federal authority.[13]

In the mid-nineteenth century, a white man named William Rogers argued that his incorporation by adoption within the Cherokee Nation exempted him from federal prosecution for the alleged murder of another white man who had similarly been adopted into the Cherokee Nation. He relied on a federal criminal law that excepted Indian against Indian crimes from federal prosecution. The Supreme Court, in *United States v. Rogers* (1846) rejected his claim, echoing the *Johnson* court's analysis on the consequences of incorporation.[14] Rogers's incorporation as a tribal member by adoption may have entitled him to "certain privileges in the tribe, and make himself amenable to their laws and usages. Yet he is not an Indian; and the exception is confined to those who by the usages and customs of the Indians are regarded as belonging to their race. It does not speak of members of a tribe, but of the race generally,—of the family of Indians; and it intended to leave them both, as regarded their own tribe, and other tribes also, to be governed by Indian usages and customs."[15] The *Rogers* opinion thus confirmed again that while tribal lands were geographically incorporated within the territories claimed by the United States, tribes nonetheless maintained an important measure of political autonomy. Importantly, the opinion offered dictum that was both gratuitous and erroneous to suggest that European governments had never acknowledged the native tribes as independent nations. "On the contrary," said the Court, "the whole continent was divided and parceled out, and granted by the governments of Europe as if it had been vacant and unoccupied land, and the Indians continually held to be, and treated as, subject to their dominion and control."[16] In similar fashion, the *Rogers* court offered a view of the tribal-federal relationship that was anchored in a highly verticalized, paternal relationship, one that accentuated the racialized discourse that was to become a staple of late nineteenth- and early twentieth-century federal Indian law jurisprudence. According to the Court, "from the very moment the general government came into existence to this time, it has exercised its power over this unfortunate race in the spirit of humanity and justice, and has endeavoured by every means in its power to enlighten their minds and increase their comforts, and to save them if possible from the consequences of their own vices."[17] Clearly, the Court was here applying a conception of dependency fundamentally at odds with the one articulated by Chief Justice John Marshall in *Worcester v. Georgia* (1832). In *Worcester,* the Court derived its understanding of dependency from principles of international law, where weaker nations allied themselves with stronger nations in order to secure protection against external threats to their territorial and political integrity. Such actions represented the *exercise*, not the *surrender*, of the tribes' sovereign national character. Conversely, the *Rogers* court relied on a sociocultural conception of dependency that viewed tribes and Indian peoples as deficient savages who were in desperate need of the benevolent support and guidance of a superior, civilized society. This narrative trope actually supported the national imaginary of a homogeneous and cohesive republican polity, since it treated culturally diverse peoples as outside the *demos* whose only hope for inclusion lay in assimilating to the norms of the dominant society as rapidly as possible. These elements of the national imaginary, buttressed by the conceptual, and evolving, twin pillars of incorporation and dependency, came together in the late nineteenth-century decision in *United States v.*

Kagama (1886),[18] the decision that ultimately gave rise to the doctrine of federal plenary power in Indian affairs.

In *United States v. Kagama*, the Supreme Court faced a constitutional challenge to the Major Crimes Act of 1885, a congressional law that purported to extend federal jurisdiction for certain enumerated crimes committed by Indians within the Indian country.[19] An Indian defendant accused of murdering an Indian victim challenged the law as beyond the scope of federal power. The jurisdictional intrusiveness of this law cannot be overstated, since it represented the first major attempt by the federal government to regulate the affairs *of* the Indians, rather than *with* the Indians. Nonetheless, attorneys for the United States argued that the law was well within the scope of federal power embodied in the Constitution's Indian Commerce Clause. First, the government argued that the 1871 Act ending treaty-making with Indian tribes had signaled, "a revolution in the policy of the government respecting Indian affairs," with the consequence that Indian tribes were no longer viewed as sovereign nations.[20] Second, the government argued that a federal criminal code for Indians constituted the regulation of commerce with the Indians under the following logic: "[I]f we have to maintain intercourse with the Indians, it is necessary and proper that they shall not be permitted to destroy each other. If they are permitted to murder each other, it is certainly an interference with [commercial] intercourse; because the number with whom intercourse will be held is thereby diminished."[21] In other words, as David Wilkins has noted, the argument attempted to portray tribal communities as islands of lawlessness and anarchy that required this level of federal intrusion to prevent the Indians from exterminating each other.[22]

The Court rejected the government's argument as a "very strained construction" of the Indian Commerce Clause.

That should have been the end of the case, since the Indian Commerce Clause represented the only textually based constitutional argument in support of this law. Instead, the Court upheld the law on the basis of a non-textually based common law argument that interwove the elements of incorporation and dependency. Federal power over Indian people, according to the Court, stemmed from federal ownership of the territories occupied by the tribes and the "right of exclusive sovereignty" that inheres in the national government: "The soil and the people within the [geographic limits of the United States] are under the political control of the government of the United States, or of the states of the Union. *There exists within the broad domain of sovereignty but these two*" (emphasis added).[23] While noting that tribal-federal political relations over the course of US history were "anomalous" and "of a complex character," the Court affirmed that tribes "were, and always have been, regarded as having a semi-independent position when they preserved their tribal relations; not as states, not as nations, not as possessed of the full attributes of sovereignty, but as a separate people, with the power of regulating their internal and social relations, and *thus far not brought under the laws of the Union or of the state within whose limits they resided*" (emphasis added).[24]

Ultimately, the Court concluded that Congress acted within its powers in passing this law. In the opinion's oft-quoted passage, the Court located the source of the federal power in the federal guardianship responsibility over its Indian dependents:

> These Indian tribes *are* the wards of the nation. They are communities *dependent* on the United States, dependent largely for their daily food; dependent for their political rights. They owe no allegiance to the states, and receive from them no protection. Because of the local ill feeling, the people of the states where

> they are found are often their deadliest enemies. From their very weakness and helplessness, so largely due to the course of dealing of the federal government with them, and the treaties in which it has been promised, there arises the duty of protection, and with it the power. This has always been recognized by the executive, and by congress, and by this court, whenever the question has arisen. (emphasis in original)[25]

From a doctrinal perspective, the *Kagama* court, as in *United States v. Rogers*, relied on a radically different conception of Indian dependency as compared to the model envisioned in *Worcester*. In *Kagama*, the Court emphasized elements of what we might call *factual dependency*, as opposed to *Worcester's* international-law-derived notion of intergovernmental or *political* dependency in the tribal-federal relationship. In noting that tribes were factually dependent upon the federal government for their daily wants, including the provision of food rations, the Court carefully omitted references to federal policies that created such dependency, including policies between 1867 and 1883 that enabled or condoned the senseless slaughter of buffalo, a main staple of Plains Indians diet and cultural life.[26]

From a constitutional perspective, the *Kagama* court recognized a non-textually based common law theory of federal power that was completely untethered from the Constitution or any other possible source of limitation, except perhaps the self-regulating fiduciary standards of a benevolent Christian guardian nation. Indeed, a close reading of the opinion suggests that the Court showed no trepidation in recognizing an unbridled federal power to empire at will in Indian country. Instead, the Court was chiefly concerned about minimizing federal interference with or intrusion upon the state's sovereign prerogative to prosecute criminal acts committed within its geographic borders.

Finally, from a historical perspective, the *Kagama* decision provided the requisite latitude for the political branches to engage in imperial nation-building at home. Just as significant, the Court's notion of federal plenary power over culturally diverse and socially normative outsiders (e.g., Indians and certain foreign national immigrants) influenced later decisions that supported national imperial designs in other parts of the world. The United States' late nineteenth- and early twentieth-century acquisition of territories like the Philippines, Puerto Rico, Alaska, and Hawaii raised the question as to whether the Constitution "followed the flag" in terms of providing the full panoply of American legal rights to the newly incorporated territories and setting limits on the federal power in its governance of such lands and peoples. The Court ultimately settled on a conception of *incorporation* to help determine the normative legal framework that would operate within a particular territory. In a series of cases known collectively as the *Insular Cases*,[27] the Court held, in basic terms, that the Constitution only followed the flag in incorporated territories. Denizens of unincorporated territories were protected only against federal intrusions on rights deemed fundamental in the constitutional sense. The designation of territories as incorporated or unincorporated essentially turned on congressional intent, which in turn, was contingent upon qualities of race and level of civilization possessed by the people in the new territories. Territories occupied by peoples regarded as savage or barbarians were typically designated as unincorporated (e.g. Philippines, Puerto Rico) while territories occupied by peoples who were regarded as more civilized were designated as incorporated (e.g., Hawaii, Alaska). The general view of the Court was that imposing the constraints of the Constitution on all newly acquired territories, without regard to the nature of the indigenous populations, might unduly hamper the nation's imperial project.[28] In the words of one of the *Insular Cases*, *Downes v. Bidwell* (1901):

> If those possessions are inhabited by alien races, differing from us in religion, customs, laws, methods of taxation and modes of thought, the administration of government and justice, according to Anglo-Saxon principles, may for a time be impossible; and the question at once arises whether large concessions ought not to be made for a time, that, ultimately, our own theories may be carried out, and the blessings of a free government under the Constitution extended to them. We decline to hold that there is anything in the Constitution to forbid such action.[29]

The exceptional judicial deference shown to the political branches in the late nineteenth and early twentieth centuries coincided with a substantial influx of immigrants to America who challenged the sociocultural and political hegemony of Anglo-Saxons. Immigrants from China, and southern and eastern Europe, were exploited for their labor but despised for their perceived un-American values, features, and aspirations. These newcomers threatened to upset the national imaginary of an Anglo-Saxon polity and helped to trigger a rash of civic organizations dedicated to reifying America's founding narrative and laws designed to curb or eliminate immigration and deport aliens who were deemed undesirable. In short, as Alexander Aleinikoff has observed, "[t]o retain Anglo-Saxon domination of American institutions, the massive migration of un-American groups had to be stanched, and those who had already gained entry had to be effectively 'Americanized'."[30]

American Indians were not spared from this cultural homogenization and assimilation campaign. Federal policy makers and private citizen groups had long advocated for the division and privatization of tribal lands, the disintegration of tribal political systems, and the wholesale incorporation of Indian people into the general fabric of American society. If anything, the calls for such policy reforms in Indian policy became more intense and urgent during the latter half of the nineteenth century. In 1868, for example, Nathaniel G. Taylor, Commissioner of Indian Affairs, advocated for an aggressive assimilation campaign for Indians built on the "successes" of the Cherokee Nation in making the transition from the savage to the civilized life. The elements of such a program included creating greater proximity between Indians and whites, circumscribing tribal territories and localizing the tribal population, and introducing agrarianism and concepts of private property, all under the watchful eye and tutelage of "the Christian teacher and missionary, moving *pari passu* with every other cause" (emphasis added).[31] Christian reformers, including those who attended the Lake Mohonk (New York) Conferences of Friends of the Indians beginning in the early 1880s, also advocated for the division of Indian lands in severalty as a step toward civilizing the Indians and preparing them for citizenship. They placed particular emphasis on policies that would lead to the "disintegration of all tribal [political] organizations," since, in their minds, political organization as tribes constituted one of the "most serious hindrances to the advancement of the Indian toward civilization."[32] The extensive entanglement between Christian denominations and the federal policy makers in the formulation and implementation of Indian policy included the appointment of Christian clergymen who served both as missionaries and as government agents to their Indian charges. If any federal officials voiced concerns about the constitutionality of such measures, in light of the First Amendment's prohibition against the establishment of religion, they were a distinct and wholly ineffective minority.[33]

The General Allotment Act of 1887[34] served as the congressional vehicle to advance the policies articulated above, notably the dissolution of tribally held communal lands in favor of individually allotted parcels, the sale of surplus Indian lands to non-Indian homesteaders, and the introduction of civilizing elements within tribal society, including agrarian forms of subsistence, the practice of Christianity, and an array of disincentives (including criminal sanctions) to move tribal members away from traditional cultural and religious practices.

In *Lone Wolf v. Hitchcock* (1903),[35] tribal citizens of the Kiowa, Comanche, and Apache Tribes challenged the allotment process on their tribal lands in present-day Oklahoma as being in violation of the rights contained in the 1867 treaty of Medicine Lodge, and by extension, in violation of their constitutional rights. In substantial measure, the case raised the issue of whether federal implementation of the allotment process required the actual consent of Indian tribes before moving forward.

The Court gave relatively short shrift to the tribes' arguments, relying heavily on *Kagama*'s notions of dependency and incorporation. According to the Court, the tribes' argument in the case "ignores the status of the contracting Indians and the relation of dependency they bore and continue to bear towards the government of the United States. To uphold the claim would be to adjudge that the indirect operation of the treaty was to materially limit and qualify the controlling authority of Congress in respect to the care and protection of the Indians, and to deprive Congress, in a possible emergency, when the necessity might be urgent for a partition and disposal of the tribal lands, of all power to act, if the assent of the Indians could not be obtained."[36]

According to the Court, Congress's power to legislate in Indian affairs included the power unilaterally to abrogate treaty guarantees made to Indian tribes. The Court noted that the power to abrogate treaty rights was subject to a soft caveat that essentially required the existence of a congressionally determined necessity before the federal government could breach faith with the Indian tribes. In the Court's words:

> The power exists to abrogate the provisions of an Indian treaty, though presumably such power will be exercised only when circumstances arise which will not only justify the government in disregarding the stipulations of the treaty, but may demand, in the interest of the country and the Indians themselves, that it should do so. When, therefore, treaties were entered into between the United States and a tribe of Indians it was never doubted that the *power* to abrogate existed in Congress, and that in a contingency such power might be availed of from considerations of governmental policy, particularly if consistent with perfect good faith towards the Indians.[37]

The Court describes the federal power in Indian affairs as "plenary" and noted that Congress has exercised such power "from the beginning."[38] This is a patently false statement. Prior to the 1871 end of treaty-making, federal Indian policy proceeded on the basis of bilateral government-to-government relations. Even the Removal Act of 1830 required the consent of the tribes to surrender their eastern homelands in exchange for lands in the Indian territory, now present-day Oklahoma.[39]

If indeed the only check on federal plenary power to abrogate treaty rights was evidence of some sort of exigency or necessity that required the federal government to break faith with the Indian tribes, what exigency or necessity existed in the *Lone Wolf* case? The Court provided an answer but only in the most oblique form. The Court explained that "as with treaties made with foreign nations (*Chinese Exclusion Case, 130 U.S. 581*), the legislative power might pass laws in conflict with treaties made with the Indians."[40] The parenthetical case is *Chae Chan Ping v. United States* (1888),[41] wherein the Court upheld Congress's unilateral abrogation of a treaty with China. Congress abrogated its treaty obligations with China largely in response to the concerns of western states, particularly California, about the massive influx of Chinese immigrants and their inability or unwillingness to acclimate or become "Americanized" in accordance with the prevailing nationalist fervor of the day. The Court's articulation of these concerns is worth reciting at length:

> The differences of race added greatly to the difficulties of the situation. Notwithstanding the favorable provisions of the new articles of the Treaty of 1868, by which all the privileges, immunities, and exemptions were extended to subjects of China in the United States which were accorded to citizens or subjects of the most favored nation, they remained strangers in the land, residing apart by themselves, and adhering to the customs and usages of their own country. It seems impossible for them to assimilate with our people or to make any change in their habits or modes of living. As they grew in numbers each year the people of the coast saw, or believed they saw, in the facility of immigration, and in the crowded millions of China, where population presses upon the means of subsistence, great danger that at no distant day that portion of our country would be overrun by them unless prompt action was taken to restrict their immigration. The people there accordingly petitioned earnestly for protective legislation.[42]

An 1879 memorial from California residents to Congress conveyed similar concerns but expressed them with a much greater sense of urgency. The Court referenced a passage from the memorial as follows:

> [T]he presence of Chinese laborers had a baneful effect upon the material interests of the State, and upon public morals; that their immigration was in numbers approaching the character of an

> Oriental invasion, and was a menace to our civilization; that they retained the habits and customs of their own country, and in fact constituted a Chinese settlement within the State, without any interest in our country or its institutions.[43]

A congressional proponent of the Chinese exclusion laws affirmatively embraced the rhetoric of American nationalism and linked it to the resurgent Anglo-Saxonism of the nineteenth century to highlight the fact that, at least from his perspective, the Chinese were simply the wrong type of immigrants for the American polity:

> No voice is raised against the immigration from across the Atlantic because we feel ourselves akin to the people who thus come to our shores. They are the offspring of the nations from which the founders of the Republic, its defenders, and heroes sprang. They are not only of our race, but allied in moral and religious sentiments, in the degree of culture attained. By contrast, the Chinaman is neither socially, nor politically fit to assimilate with us.[44]

The *Lone Wolf* court's parenthetical reference to *Chae Chan Ping* suggests that the exigency or necessity for breaking faith with the Indian tribes was their very insistence on maintaining distinct cultural and political systems and their refusal to surrender their indigeneity to the forces of assimilation and American nationalism that were engulfing them. Their assertion of extant treaty rights represented a last stand against domestic imperialism and the resulting suppression of the formative ethos of legal pluralism. The bandwidth for acceptable forms of cultural pluralism in the late nineteenth and early twentieth centuries was exceedingly low; the tolerance for any forms of legal pluralism during the same period seemed to be nil.

In 1924, Congress enacted the Indian Citizenship Act that unilaterally conferred (some say *imposed*) US citizenship upon all American Indians who were not already citizens, with the proviso that the Act would not disturb or impair their rights to tribal or other property.[45] The Act, in effect, accorded a form of dual citizenship for Indian people as members of the national polity and as continuing members of their tribal nations. This served to preserve a measure of political exceptionalism for Indian people that was not altogether helpful or favorable. The law constituted a form of partial (and nonconsensual) incorporation of Indian citizens that, in the words of Kevin Bruyneel, "affirmed dual citizenship status as well as citizen-ward status. Taken alone or together, the dual citizenship and citizen-ward interpretations of the [Indian Citizenship Act] show that from the U.S. perspective indigenous people were neither fully inside nor fully outside the American polity."[46] In short, Indian people continued to occupy a liminal space of citizenship. As individual American citizens, they could now claim and assert as against the national government all the rights of their fellow citizens. In their capacity as citizens of their tribal nations, however, they continued to live within the shadows of the omnipresent national guardian.

The tide shifted ever so slightly in the tribes' favor in the early 1930s with the end of the allotment policies and the introduction of a policy of tribal reorganization. Felix Cohen, a lawyer/philosopher and devotee of legal pluralism (as we will see further below), along with John Collier, Commissioner of Indian Affairs and others, provided the intellectual firepower for the government's efforts to revise, at least in some ways, the political architecture of national and tribal relations and powers. In the field of federal Indian law, Cohen is perhaps best known for his authorship in 1941 of the *Handbook of Federal Indian Law*, the first sustained effort to bring coherence and structure to the field. Cohen joined the Department of the Interior in 1933 as an assistant solicitor and in that capacity, he helped draft the Indian Reorganization Act of 1934,[47] as well as a seminal US Solicitor's opinion on the powers of Indian tribes issued in 1934[48] under the name of his boss, Solicitor Nathan Margold.[49] In addition to these important texts, Cohen also drafted in 1934 a document entitled "Basic Memorandum on Drafting of Tribal Constitutions," a document that only recently has been brought to light and presented with published commentary by David Wilkins.[50] Both the Solicitor's Opinion and the Basic Memorandum reveal important aspects of the prevailing federal ideological and doctrinal understanding of tribal-federal relations and the nature of tribal sovereign powers. They warrant further consideration in brief detail.

Cohen's draft opinion on the powers of Indian tribes was developed in order to clarify a provision of the Indian Reorganization Act that authorized the constitutional reorganization of tribal governments. A requisite in drafting tribal constitutions was an understanding of the nature and scope of extant tribal powers. Cohen's opinion noted that the "most basic principle of all Indian law" is the principle that "those powers which are lawfully vested in an Indian tribe are not, in general, delegated powers granted by express acts of Congress, but rather inherent powers of a limited sovereignty which has never been extinguished. Each Indian tribe begins its relationship with the Federal Government as a sovereign power, recognized as such in treaty and legislation." Inherent tribal powers were limited by treaties with the federal government or by acts of Congress, but any power "not expressly limited remains within the domain of tribal sovereignty." The opinion, regrettably, endorses the view that "conquest" subjects tribes to the legislative power of the United States. The view is regrettable in that it is false as historical fact; most tribes were never "conquered" by the United States, at least in the militarized notion of the term. The view is also regrettable from an ideological perspective, since it reifies the mythologized superior power of Congress that, as the review above suggests, was premised upon a racialized view of Indian peoples as inferior, savage, and helpless. Nonetheless, the opinion embraces the view that conquest places tribes in a subordinated position in relation to the federal power. As a consequence, the opinion concludes, tribes' *external powers of sovereignty*—understood as the power to engage in foreign relations with other nations—were terminated; however, the tribes' *internal powers of sovereignty*—understood as the power of local self-government—were preserved. We shall have more to say shortly about the internal/external binary as employed by the Supreme Court to determine the scope of inherent tribal sovereign powers.

Cohen's Basic Memorandum on the drafting of tribal constitutions has a more enigmatic history. Even at the time of its production in 1934, it was uncertain whether or to what extent the memorandum saw the light of day beyond its use as an in-house reference to aid federal officials in reviewing draft tribal constitutions submitted for approval. In any event, the document reveals remarkably detailed knowledge about and sensitive appreciation for the diversity of indigenous forms of political organization. Furthermore, it reflects Cohen's appreciation for and commitment to principles of cultural and legal pluralism in its suggestion that tribes ought to adapt forms of government that not only responded to the exigencies of the modern era but also gave voice to their traditional indigenous notions of legitimate governance, to the extent practicable. In its introduction, for example, the memorandum advises against sending "canned" constitutions to tribes, first, because no single constitution could anticipate or properly accommodate the diversity of tribal interests, values, and traditional forms of governance that existed in the country, and second, because a model constitution so adopted by a tribe "would be only an adopted child and not the natural offspring of Indian hearts and minds."[51]

The memorandum's section on political leadership, titled "Place of Chiefs in Tribal Government," recognizes the wisdom of developing contemporary forms of governance and leadership that are congruent with the traditional cultural and social norms of the tribal community. Indeed, the contemporary literature on tribal economic development suggests that congruence or "cultural match" between traditional values and contemporary forms of self-governance is the leading contributor to positive and sustained economic growth in Indian country.[52] In circumstances where the traditional modes for selecting political leaders contain elements of secrecy, the memorandum offers suggestions on how tribes might preserve such practices while accommodating expectations for greater transparency in government: "Where the traditional methods of appointing new chiefs or removing old chiefs are still known and respected and are still practicable, it should be possible to state in the tribal constitutions in simple language what this method is. If this method involves secret matters, it would be enough to provide that the chiefs or caciques should be chosen or deposed according to the ancient customs of the tribe, and that any dispute that may arise over those matters should be finally settled by the tribal court, by the tribal council, or by some other designated body."[53]

One final section of the Basic Memorandum deserves mention and discussion. The section entitled "Powers of Tribal Self-Government" opens with a declaration about the pivotal importance of this section of a tribal constitution; "[i]n effect, this statement will be a declaration of independence for the Indian tribe." This is followed by a rather stunning paragraph that not only acknowledges the intrusion of federal law into the lives of tribal communities but also attests to the illegitimacy of such intrusion in many instances. According to the Basic Memorandum,

> [t]he whole history of the Indian Office has been one of continued encroachment upon the affairs of the tribe. One after another, the powers exercised by the authorities of the tribe for the government and guidance of their people have been taken over by the Indian Office, sometimes in accordance with treaties or legislation, *but more often without any such authority*. It will be one of the chief functions of any tribal constitution to reassert and reestablish the ancient powers of the tribe except insofar as those powers have been definitely ended by federal law or have been utterly inapplicable in modern life. (emphasis added)[54]

The memorandum contemplates that tribal powers of self-government will extend primarily to members and in many instances, to non-Indians as well, particularly in the civil and regulatory contexts. With respect to criminal justice, the memorandum specifies that tribes "must leave to the federal court the problem of punishing non-Indians who commit offenses against Indians."[55] This is an interesting formulation of the problem, since it does not state that tribes actually lack the jurisdictional power to prosecute non-Indians. Deferring to federal authorities for the prosecution of non-Indians may have been the consequence of perceived deficits in tribal law enforcement capacity, and not jurisdictional authority per se. In any event, the memorandum only allows tribal governments to detain non-Indian offenders and turn them over to federal authorities.

While some scholars have criticized the so-called *Indian New Deal* policies of the 1930s for encouraging a "kinder and gentler" form of tribal assimilation (e.g., republican forms of government, corporatized business structures, inducements to engage in widespread natural resource development, etc.), they cannot deny that at least on ideological grounds, the federal Indian policies of the period helped to resuscitate tribal sovereignty as a viable force within the realm of national politics. To be sure, tribal leaders and advocates of tribal sovereignty played an immeasurably significant role in maintaining their systems of self-government throughout the dark years of allotment; without their sustained efforts to nurture the flames of sovereignty, there would have been nothing for the progressive federal actors of Cohen's era to revive.

For Felix Cohen, however, the project of Indian reorganization went far beyond working to halt the devastating consequences of the allotment era. The work resonated strongly with his commitment to legal pluralism and his belief that the empowerment of individuals working through collectivities of various forms could help redress the inequities in society, particularly the disparities in economic well-being. In much the same vein as Will Kymlicka's notion of culture as a "context of choice," legal pluralists like Cohen believed that groups or associations were "fora where individuals could pursue particular values, subject only to a general economic and political scheme. The role of the state and the legal system was to guarantee that individuals could associate with others to pursue their needs and that no one association or collective entity could use its power to oppress individuals who belonged to other groups (oppression being defined, at least initially, as economic oppression)."[56] In Cohen's formulation of legal pluralism, the autonomy of collectivities (e.g., unions, corporations, Indian tribes, etc.) was subject to an overarching national planning effort that would help coordinate, rather than direct, the work of the groups. This ideological understanding of national power may help place into proper context Cohen's views about federal power in Indian affairs. For Cohen, collectivities represented the aggregate of commonly held individual values that, in turn, formed the constitutive elements of the broader society and indeed, the state itself. In the context of Indian affairs, Cohen envisioned the tribe functioning in the manner of a private corporation with public responsibilities to help improve conditions on the ground in Indian country.[57] The bureaucracy of the federal Indian Service would support, but not necessarily dictate, the tribe's institution-building and agenda-setting efforts.

The flaw in Cohen's conceptual formulation, as discussed in Dalia Mitchell's biography of Cohen, was to view Indian tribes as just another form of collective. His growing awareness and appreciation for tribes as distinct culture groups with unique, and sometimes disparate, values and conceptions of the good required a major adjustment in Cohen's pluralist thinking. His draft opinion on the Powers of Indian Tribes (1934), for example, reflected some of this revised thinking but perhaps not enough to make a substantial difference for Indian tribes. As Mitchell suggests, Cohen's deep immersion in Western political philosophy likely prevented him from straying too far from the canonical features of government and its attendant bureaucracies and led him to focus on mediating political power in service of the public good. According to Mitchell, the Powers of the Indian Tribes opinion, as well as the Indian New Deal itself, lacked "a deeper understanding of the multiplicity of legal cultures and legal values that characterized modern American society. Cohen intuitively sensed this flaw, even though he could not fully explain it."[58]

Notwithstanding these limitations, Cohen's regular interaction with Indian tribes and their leaders did cause him to revise substantially his conception of legal pluralism during the course of his years in the Indian Service. For example, Cohen's earlier belief in the capacity of the unitary national polity to accommodate a multiplicity of interests and their associated values systems was reflected in a pluralist model he called *systematic pluralism*. The model envisioned a scheme of gradual social integration by which group differences would eventually disappear over the course of time, where the many would become one. According to Mitchell, Cohen drafted the *Handbook of Federal Indian Law* with the conceptual model of systematic pluralism as its ideological underpinning.[59] By the mid-1940s, Cohen recognized the limitations inherent in this pluralist model, due in part to his growing recognition of the sociocultural dissonance between indigenous and mainstream American values and the likelihood that suppression of those values in the model of systematic pluralism would effectively doom the existence of the group, or in this case, tribe. He therefore shifted to a pluralist model that envisioned a structural arrangement between distinct value systems wherein the polities would be in constant dialogue with each other in an effort to articulate and mediate conflicting values. This model of *comparative pluralism*, akin to Duncan Ivison's *institutional design* approach, served as the ideological underpinning for Cohen's work on the development and operation of the Indian Claims Commission established by the Indian Claims Commission Act of 1946 to resolve tribal claims cases against the federal government.[60] According to Mitchell, the ICCA carried great symbolic value for Cohen: "Intellectually, he believed that the establishment of an investigatory commission—rather than an adversarial body—to hear and determine tribal land claims against the federal government would illustrate the importance of agency and the possibility of communication and translation between and among distinct value systems."[61]

From Mitchell's assessment, Cohen failed to accomplish most of what he had set out to do in Indian country, in part because of quotidian bureaucratic entanglements and political disagreements about the shape and direction of the Indian New Deal, and in part because of ideological tension with the predominate political philosophy of the day, liberalism. In Mitchell's words, Cohen's efforts revealed the limits of "using a legal system predicated upon individualism to remedy past injuries to diverse communities." In addition, she notes that "[s]imilar constraints continue to impede contemporary attempts to devise a plural polity, as different others (ethnic, religious, cultural, and political groups) struggle both to escape law's violence and to come under its protection."[62]

Ever the optimist, Cohen probably would concur with Mitchell's summary assessment of his work:

> Cohen's gradual realization of the law's limits illustrates how in the shadows of the law lurks hope, as constraints may be transformed into possibilities. For those who seek to create a pluralist polity and for those who are affected by such attempts, the law can help facilitate social contacts. Even failed attempts to devise formalistic legal structures to accomplish pluralistic goals create peripheries where pluralism might flourish. Our treatment of different groups and individuals, as Cohen so aptly described it, is the litmus test of our democracy; it reflects 'a set of beliefs that forms the intellectual equipment of a generation.' In the shadows of the law, doubt may turn to hope.[63]

As noted above, the federal policies of Indian reorganization, and Cohen's intellectual contributions to those efforts, helped to create the ideological, political, and juridical space within which tribal leaders could (re)build their systems of indigenous self-government in accordance with their value systems. Unfortunately, this window of opportunity was short-lived as federal Indian policy in the post–World War II era once again emphasized the goal of sociopolitical incorporation of American Indians into the fabric of American society.[64] The rhetoric and policy of *termination* reified the ideological position of the allotment era in viewing wardship status for Indians as an albatross around the necks of individual Indians, hindering their efforts to assimilate into the broader society. In this updated version of social reengineering for indigenous peoples, the urban landscape replaced the farm homestead as the locus for the remaking of Indian society. Federal policy encouraged individual Indian citizens to leave their Indian country homes and chart new personal destinies in urban America.[65]

The ambivalence in the national commitment toward tribal sovereignty, and more broadly, to a legally plural society, is reflected in the Supreme Court's opinion from this era, *Williams v. Lee* (1959).[66] In holding that state courts had no jurisdiction to hear a Navajo reservation-based contract dispute between Navajo Indian debtors and a non-Indian creditor, the Court paired the following two sentences and linked them together by a reference to the Indian Reorganization Act: "Not satisfied solely with centralized government of Indians, [Congress] encouraged tribal governments and courts to become stronger and more highly organized. See, *e.g.,* the Wheeler-Howard Act [IRA]. Congress has followed a policy calculated eventually to make all Indians full-fledged participants in American society."[67] Superficially, at least, the sentences announce policy statements that are at war with each other. On closer inspection, however, the Court's language reflects Felix Cohen's notion of systematic pluralism, the idea that an enlarged and unitary national polity could be fashioned to accommodate multiple interests and value systems, with tribal governments seen not as political competitors with the state, but as collectives through which indigenous values can be expressed and made meaningful in the lives of Indian people. Recall that in Cohen's conception of this model of legal pluralism, the federal government serves as the centralized national planning center to help coordinate the work of the various collectives that make up the society. The *Williams* court seems to echo that view of national power as well when it states that the "[f]ederal government's power over Indians is derived from Art. I, Section 8, clause 3, of the United States Constitution and from the necessity of giving uniform protection to a dependent people. *United States v. Kagama, supra.*"[68]

The last element of the *Williams* case worth highlighting here is the Court's application of the external/internal binary for describing the scope of inherent tribal sovereignty, as featured in the Power of Indian Tribes Solicitor's Opinion of 1934. Recall that the Solicitor's opinion characterized the tribes' *external powers of sovereignty* as the power to engage in foreign relations with other nations, while the tribes' *internal powers of sovereignty* were understood as the power of local self-government. After reviewing the history of treaty relations between the federal government and the Navajo Nation, the *Williams* court concluded that the contracting parties understood that "the *internal* affairs of the Indians remained exclusively within the jurisdiction of whatever tribal government existed" (emphasis added).[69] The Court's understanding of *internal* seems clearly to suggest a territorial conception of self-government, with the tribe's power extending to all activities and all persons (including non-Indians) acting within the tribe's juridical space: "It is immaterial that respondent is not an Indian. He was on the Reservation and the transaction with an Indian took place there. The cases in this Court have consistently guarded the authority of Indian governments *over their reservations*" (emphasis added).[70]

Despite ruling against the state, *Williams* is actually known for creating wider openings for the application of state law in Indian country. The *Cherokee Nation* cases of the 1830s were understood as creating an impenetrable barrier to state law unless Congress explicitly authorized the intrusion. In *Williams,* the assumption seems to be reversed; state law may apply in Indian country unless Congress has stated otherwise or the application of state law would infringe on tribal rights of self-government. Notwithstanding this legal result, the jurisprudential legacy of *Williams* is that it helped to resuscitate tribal sovereignty as a viable force within the realm of national politics.[71]

To conclude this review of the Court's treatment of *incorporation* and *dependency* in its federal Indian law cases, we look at *United States v. Wheeler* (1978), a case decided just over two weeks after the *Oliphant* decision was handed down.[72] In *Wheeler,* the Court upheld the inherent power of Indian tribes to prosecute their own tribal members. While the Court reiterated the statements in *Oliphant* about the jurisdictional consequences of the tribe's incorporation within the United States' territory, it spoke with greater precision about the scope of the tribe's inherent sovereign powers utilizing the now-familiar external/internal binary formulation from its earlier precedents. The Court's analysis is worth restating in full:

> [T]he sovereign power of a tribe to prosecute its members for tribal offenses clearly does not fall within that part of sovereignty which the Indians implicitly lost by virtue of their dependent status. The areas in which such implicit divestiture of sovereignty has been held to have occurred are those involving the relations between an Indian tribe and nonmembers of the tribe. Thus, Indian tribes can no longer freely alienate to non-Indians the land they occupy. They cannot enter into direct commercial or governmental relations with foreign nations. And, as we have recently held, they cannot try nonmembers in tribal courts.
>
> These limitations rest on the fact that the dependent status of Indian tribes within our territorial jurisdiction is necessarily inconsistent with their freedom independently to determine their external relations. But the powers of self-government, including

> the power to prescribe and enforce internal criminal laws, are of a different type. They involve only the relations among members of a tribe. Thus, they are not such powers as would necessarily be lost by virtue of a tribe's dependent status. '[T]he settled doctrine of the law of nations is, that a weaker power does not surrender its independence—its right to self-government, by associating with a stronger, and taking its protection.' *Worcester v. Georgia, supra*, at 560–561.[73]

In these passages, the Court dramatically shifts the focus of the external/internal binary toward the localized reservation population of Indians and non-Indians. In other words, the Court totally eschews the *Williams* court's territorial approach that considered matters occurring within the reservation territory, including those involving non-Indians, to be a function of *internal relations*, and thus, embraced within the scope of the tribe's sovereignty. In *Wheeler*, internal relations are interpreted to mean intra-tribal relations. External relations are those involving non-Indians or non-members; the Court, oddly, uses the terms interchangeably. Earlier in the opinion, the Court acknowledged that Indian tribes are "a good deal more than 'private, voluntary organizations,'"[74] although the *Wheeler* court's application of the external/internal binary begs the question of just how much more.

The citation to *Worcester v. Georgia* at the end of the quoted passage from *Wheeler* is almost tragi-comic in effect, since the language that precedes it substantially denudes the moral force of *Worcester*'s reference to tribal self-government. It was in *Worcester* wherein the Court emphasized that federal treaties and acts "manifestly consider the several Indian nations as distinct political communities, having territorial boundaries, within which their authority is exclusive, and having a right to all the lands within those boundaries, which is not only acknowledged, but guarantied by the United States."[75]

Clearly, the Court has come a long way from its position in *Worcester v. Georgia*. Its evolving conceptions of *incorporation* and *dependency* have substantially narrowed the geopolitical spaces within which tribal sovereignty can operate. At the same time, these developments have contributed to the Court's arrogation of substantial, unprecedented power to impose its own imperial designs onto Indian tribes when responding to challenges about the nature and scope of tribal sovereign powers. The contemporary environment in the federal judiciary is, therefore, inclined to resist any expansion of the powers of Indian tribes even as the political branches continue to respond favorably to tribal claims for increasingly more robust forms of self-determination. Getting the Court to loosen its ideological tethers around the concepts of incorporation and dependency will likely require moving outside the domain of federal Indian law doctrine or beyond legal doctrine generally. We turn to consider briefly one such alternative domain, the ideological history of US federalism, as a possible source to nudge the Court off its current track.

Incorporation and the Ideology of US Federalism

In her book, *The Ideological Origins of American Federalism* (2010),[76] Alison LaCroix traces the antecedents of American federalist thought by examining pre-1780s theoretical political discourse and institutional practices, both in Europe and in colonial America, relating to polycentric governance systems. She summarizes the central arguments of the book in these words:

> [T]he debates of the 1760s through the 1780s culminated in a new constitutionalization of federalism, a process that continued into the 1800s. From a disconnected and sometimes ambiguous

> set of arguments about divided sovereignty in politics, American colonists and early republicans fashioned a new architecture of legal and constitutional authority built on a subject-matter division of governmental power. In contrast to earlier systems—whether formal or informal—of polycentric government, the federalism of the late eighteenth- and early nineteenth-century United States was specifically designed to avoid the ancient problem of *imperium in imperio*, or dominion within a dominion, that had so troubled the British Atlantic political world for decades. The significant innovation of the American federal idea was to authorize the division of sovereignty and to create viable legal categories that could contain multiple sources of governmental power within one overarching system.[77]

The point in highlighting LaCroix's project at this juncture is not principally to critique the major premises of her argument or to challenge her interpretation of certain historical events in terms of their political or ideological significance; no less imposing a figure as historian Gordon Wood has already done that.[78] We will examine some of their major points of disagreement in due course, but for the moment, I want to focus attention on two particular strands of political thought that LaCroix contends informed the discourse of American federalism. The first strand focuses on seventeenth- and eighteenth-century Scottish political theories of union that challenged the prevailing British model of legal centralism. The second strand focuses on eighteenth-century colonial theories of divided government that purported to organize political power along the axis of an external/internal model of distributive sovereignty.

Turning now to the first strand of political thought, LaCroix contends that the history of Anglo-Scottish union during the seventeenth and eighteenth centuries served as fertile ground for theorists on both sides of the ocean to consider the forms of political unions and their implications for sovereignty. For about a century, 1603–1707, Scotland and England were joined under a *union of crowns*, where the nations shared a common monarch but preserved their distinctive parliaments and hence, their sovereign authority. The 1707 Act of Union dissolved the Scottish and English Parliaments, creating in their place a unified British Parliament that exercised sovereignty over the unitary body politic. According to LaCroix, "studies from the years before 1707 generated theories of union that later reappeared in the American context; moreover, the analyses provided historical examples of alternative approaches to union and empire that challenged the official British account of an empire based on unitary parliamentary sovereignty."[79]

Scottish and British political theorists distinguished between *federal* and *incorporating* forms of union, where the critical element was the nature and degree of political autonomy (i.e., sovereignty) preserved by the contracting bodies politic following the union. LaCroix offers the more detailed descriptions of federal and incorporating unions developed by Scottish nationalist James Hodges. According to Hodges, these are the features of a *federal* or *confederate* union:

> [T]hat whereby Distinct, Free, and Independent Kingdoms, Dominions or States, do unite their separate Interests into one common Interest, for the mutual benefit of both, so far as relates to certain Conditions and Articles agreed upon betwixt them, retaining in the mean time their several Independencies, National Distinctions, and the different Laws, Customs, and Government of each.[80]

In contrast, Hodges describes an *incorporating* union as follows:

> The Title of an Incorporating Union denotes that Kind, where by distinct and independent Kingdoms and Dominions parting with

> their distinction, and Independency do so unite themselves with another Kingdom, as to be embodied with it, and to become a particular Part, Province, or District of the Kingdom with which they do so unite, being subject to the Laws and Government thereof.[81]

LaCroix makes clear that incorporating unions were often associated with empire building and/or conquest whereby weaker nations were subsumed by larger, more powerful ones. Confederated or federal alliances, on the other hand, were characterized by relative parity, independence, and equality among the contracting nations. Empiring nations like England approached the matter of unions with a decided bias in favor of incorporation, with the superior sovereignty residing in the British Parliament and all members of the newly enlarged body politic subject to unitary British law.

Participants in the American debates on forms of confederation during the 1770s frequently invoked the Scottish-English union example, particularly in the context of determining the representation of states in the new union and highlighting the potential hazards of entrenching too much power in the larger states. As LaCroix demonstrates, the Scottish-English experience of 1707 carried significant meaning for those charged with organizing the newly emerging American nation: "If the lesson of 1707 demonstrated anything to participants in the American debates of the 1770s, it was that a state with imperial aspirations would not easily consent to a truly federal association with another, less powerful state. Thus, although a federated union might be possible, a federated empire was unlikely to thrive. For the fledgling association of the former American colonies, then, the difference between empire and union was profound."[82]

The second strand of political thought that informed the discourse of American federalism, according to LaCroix, is the eighteenth-century colonial notion of divided government where political power is organized along the axis of an external/internal model of distributive sovereignty. American colonists employed this conception of divided government to challenge British Parliamentary Acts, particularly British tax laws that were perceived as intruding beyond the ambiguous boundaries that separated the spheres of colonial and parliamentary authority. Among the examples LaCroix offers of this rhetorical strategy are the writings of Daniel Dulany, a lawyer and colonial official who mounted strong opposition to the British Parliament's Stamp Act of 1765. This deeply controversial tax measure ignited fierce opposition from colonists and helped to define the principles by which colonists articulated their opposition to British rule. LaCroix suggests that Dulany interwove notions of colonial dependency with the external/internal binary to help clarify the appropriate spheres of authority for both colonial governments and the British Parliament: "By their Constitutions of Government," wrote Dulany, "the Colonies are impowered to impose internal Taxes. This Power is compatible with their Dependence.... May not then the Line be distinctly and justly drawn between such Acts as are necessary, or proper, for preserving or securing the Dependence of the Colonies, and such as are not necessary or proper for that very important Purpose; and would moreover Destroy the fundamental and necessary Principle of Constitutional Liberty?"[83] By that measure, according to LaCroix, colonial acts that "might threaten the hierarchy of the empire" would necessarily be preempted by the authority of the British Parliament.[84]

LaCroix's scholarship makes clear that these concepts—incorporation, dependency, external and internal powers of governance—were not only well known among the colonial leaders of the revolutionary era, but were employed regularly and strategically in the political discourse of the day to advance arguments in support of divided government between the colonies and the central government in Great Britain. As applied in the context of tribal-federal relations, and in light of the language of the Constitution, the adoption of treaty-making as the mechanism for conducting tribal-federal intergovernmental relations, and the early jurisprudence of the Supreme Court relating to tribal affairs, it is unlikely that either the early American political leaders or the leaders of the tribal nations envisioned their alliances to be in the nature of an incorporating union. The *closer* model to describe the tribal-federal alliances or form of union, although it is hardly a perfect fit, is the confederal or federal model of union, wherein each distinct body politic remains substantially independent of the other and retains its sovereign authority to govern within its respective sphere. The experience of the Scottish-English union of 1707 highlights the hazards for a federal union when one of the contracting states has imperial aspirations, as the Indian tribes in the United States have come to understand all too well. For Indian tribes, the challenge, both historically and in the modern era, is holding fast to the conceptual model of the federal union and preventing the slide toward the incorporating union model. Despite the declarations in cases like *Oliphant* and *Wheeler* that the incorporation of Indian tribes is a fait accompli, it is clear that even those decisions acknowledge, perhaps begrudgingly, the ongoing vitality and independence of tribal sovereignty. Indeed, restating one of *Oliphant*'s core passages will reveal just how closely the Court's statement of intergovernmental relations tracks the argument by Dulany noted above:

> Upon incorporation into the territory of the United States, the Indian tribes thereby come under the territorial sovereignty of

> the United States and their exercise of separate power is constrained so as not to conflict with the interests of this overriding sovereignty.[85]

As I have noted in my earlier writing, this formulation of the implicit divestiture doctrine is quite different conceptually and practically from the Court's earlier pronouncement describing the various means by which inherent tribal powers are divested.[86] In the paragraph immediately preceding the one quoted above, the *Oliphant* court notes that Indian tribes are prohibited from exercising powers that are "inconsistent with their status" as domestic dependent nations.[87] The Court offers no guidance for how lower courts are to interpret the meaning of powers that are "inconsistent with their status" nor does it explain why this normative threshold is even appropriate for assessing the viability of various tribal powers. On the other hand, assessing the continuing viability of inherent tribal powers in relation to the interests of the overriding federal sovereignty lends itself to a more determinant analysis in the sense that facts and evidence could be marshaled to identify the respective interests of the sovereigns and to ascertain the potential areas of conflict. This approach, like Dulany's arguments to his colonial audiences, respects the overriding political authority and power of the general government, not because of any notion of inherent social or cultural superiority, but out of deference to the subjects of governmental action that are more appropriately left to its general administration and control.

LaCroix contends that the scheme of dividing authority on the basis of the subject matter of governmental action was the precise ideological innovation that informed American federalism and helped overcome the conceptual and practical challenges of *imperium in imperio,* or state within a state. Historian Gordon Wood challenges this central premise of

LaCroix's work by suggesting that all the leading revolutionary figures actually accepted the logic of the unitary sovereign; they simply relocated it and entrenched it within the people, whose long experience in America with divided government operating at multiple levels prepared them for life in a federalist state. Citing the writing of Founder James Wilson, Wood notes that "[s]overeignty always stayed with the people at large; '[t]hey can delegate it in such proportions, to such bodies, on such terms, and under such limitations, as they think proper'. For this reason, Wilson noted, the people 'can distribute one portion of power to the more contracted circle called State governments: they can also furnish another proportion to the government of the United States'."[88]

The attraction of Wood's critique, and by extension, a possible flaw in LaCroix's work, is his implicit recognition that "the people" who were deemed to possess the ultimate sovereign authority during the revolutionary era were a fairly homogenous bunch who also conceived of themselves as one *demos*. Adding the history of tribal nations to this mix would have certainly complicated the analysis of federalism but it would have provided the occasion for examining the extent to which the colonists were prepared to apply their own arguments for independent spheres of political autonomy to the situation of the Indian tribes.

Indians do make an appearance in Wood's critique, as well as in LaCroix's book, albeit in the endnotes of her book. In fact, Wood opens his critique of LaCroix's book with a story about Indian tribes. He notes that following one of his lectures on the First Congress, "a very angry woman" asked, "Why don't you historians of the Founders give proper credit to the Iroquois in the creation of the Constitution?" The angry woman, it turns out, was Laura Nader, an anthropologist at Berkeley and sister of consumer advocate Ralph

Nader. Wood gives a brief, somewhat dismissive, overview of Nader's argument about the Iroquois and their purported contributions to the Constitution and then, turning to LaCroix's book, faults her for giving this story more credit than it deserves. "The Iroquois," said Wood, "and other Indians certainly contributed a great deal to early American culture, but ideas about federalism were not among their contributions." Later in his critique, while describing the colonists' long experience with divided government, Wood states, "Americans from the outset were conditioned to think of political authority as very different from the top-down hierarchical structures of England and Europe. The early colonists did not need the Indians or anyone else to tell them how to dole out and divide up political power and construct confederations."[89]

To her credit—and to Wood's great dismay—LaCroix acknowledges the scholarly debate about whether the Iroquois Confederacy served as a model for the early colonial plans for confederation and she cites some of the most prominent scholarly literature on both sides of the issue. She concludes however, almost with regret, "[O]n balance, the consensus appears to be that although British North Americans were certainly aware of the confederal nature of Iroquois government, the case for causation has not been made."[90]

One of those North Americans who was certainly aware of the Iroquois Confederation was Benjamin Franklin, a fact noted by LaCroix. Franklin wrote in 1751, referring to the Iroquois: "It would be a very strange thing if six nations of ignorant savages should be capable of forming a scheme for such an union, and be able to execute it in such a manner as that it has subsisted for ages, and appears indissoluble; and yet that a like union should be impracticable for ten or a dozen English colonies, to whom it is more necessary, and must be more advantageous."[91] Likewise, in his 1787 study of world governments, *Defence of the Constitutions of Government of the United States,* John Adams urged the leading colonial political leaders to give due attention to the Indians' government structures, particularly their ideas about a separation of political powers and an institutional legislative structure that was so democratic, "the real sovereignty resided in the body of the people."[92]

In the final analysis, the LaCroix-Wood exchanges as they relate to indigenous contributions to American democracy and federalism reveal the missed opportunity to engage seriously with indigenous understandings of the historico-legal relationship with citizens of the settler state. Such missed opportunities may mean little or nothing to members of the dominant society, but they carry immense implications for indigenous peoples whose claims to sovereignty are intimately enmeshed in the history of indigenous-Euro-American relations. And, as Dale Turner reminds us, "history is the main source for understanding the complex nature of Aboriginal forms of political sovereignty."[93]

Turner's work highlights the importance of unpacking the meaning of *incorporation* as it relates to indigenous claims of sovereignty within liberal democracies. Liberal theorists like Will Kymlicka may (and often do) acknowledge, for example, that indigenous societies (whom he regards as national minorities) were often incorporated within settler states in unjust ways (e.g., through outright takings or conquest of indigenous lands, unlawful settlement by non-Indians, nonconsensual transfers of indigenous lands from one empiring nation to another, or application of associated legal doctrines that subordinated or eviscerated indigenous claims to property and/or sovereign authority). On this view of incorporation, liberals contend, the state may be obliged to redress historic wrongs in the form of special rights for indigenous peoples, though these rectificatory acts must be tempered by liberalism's commitments to equality for all citizens and the limits of justice. For example, indigenous claims to property and/or sovereignty may be filtered through the liberal lens of distributive justice whereby the state recognizes differential rights of citizenship but only to the extent such rights address and rectify some perceived disadvantage experienced by members of the indigenous group. Turner suggests that this understanding of incorporation and liberalism's response thereto risks limiting indigenous rights in ahistorical ways, since it "misrecognizes the source of their right of governance."[94] An illustration of this liberal constraint in operation may help clarify the argument. During the late 1990s, non-Indian citizens in Connecticut objected strenuously to the efforts of the Connecticut-based Mashantucket Pequot tribe to enlarge their reservation's land base. A regional magazine article articulated the concerns of the non-Indian residents in the following words: "The residents who oppose annexation don't see reverence for ancestral streams and woods in the Pequot's' quest for a bigger reservation. They see simple greed, a rich tribe using a flawed federal policy to get richer."[95] The same magazine article noted similar objections by Senator Joseph Lieberman (Independent, Connecticut): "Tribes like the Pequot have reached the point where land annexation is not about preserving a culture or achieving self-sufficiency. It is about expansion of an already successful business in a way that harms their neighbors."[96] Framing the issue as "annexation" implies that the tribe's actions here operate in fairly unilateral ways, with little or no constraints imposed by federal or state law. On the contrary, the process of acquiring title to lands and placing them into trust for an Indian tribe—the formal mechanism by which Indian country is actually augmented—is onerous, time-consuming, and heavily contingent upon state consultation and acquiescence.[97] Most significant, the "lands into trust" process essentially requires Indian tribes to surrender their ownership interests in newly acquired lands in favor of a title held in trust for them by the federal government as the price for growing the tribal estate and having it recognized as "Indian country." Far from harming their non-Indian neighbors, the lands into trust process actually functions as an assault on the dignity of tribal governments by requiring them implicitly to acknowledge their dependency upon the federal government.

A *state-centered view of incorporation* necessarily yields a limited remedy for indigenous claims to property and sovereignty, since the state, even assuming it is prepared to acknowledge the illegitimacy of its founding origins, will be predisposed to respond to indigenous claims in minimalist terms. An *indigenous-centered view of incorporation*, on the other hand, offers greater potential for the state (and its actors) to recognize and act upon the truth behind the claims asserted by indigenous peoples. Again, Turner's work illuminates the critical importance of approaching these claims from the perspective of indigenous peoples:

> [M]any Aboriginal communities maintain that they are *still* self-governing nations and that they have not in fact relinquished or ceded all of their powers to the state. Aboriginal incorporation calls into question our understandings of Aboriginal peoples' political relationship with the [state]. From this perspective, Aboriginal rights of governance can be recognized in a much deeper sense than in the first interpretation. This is because Aboriginal sovereignty does not have to dissipate after the formation of the [state]; more importantly, it lies in the forefront of any current discussion about Aboriginal rights. (emphasis in original)[98]

Our collective failure to engage actively, fully and truthfully with indigenous understandings of incorporation, and more broadly, with indigenous claims to sovereignty, will leave us ill-prepared to challenge the *meta-narrative* of tribal-federal relations that continues to hold sway within federal Indian law jurisprudence. Within these narratives, Indian peoples exist in perpetuity as juridical children, subject to the ongoing and unrelenting control and dominance of a self-appointed guardian. In this legal landscape, the federal impulse to empire in Indian affairs continues to operate with few tangible constraints. Tribal sovereignty is perceived as malleable, accordion-like, and subject to modification at the whim of the sovereign. Tribal people exist within a liminal space that is both within the controlling grip of the law, and yet outside of its protective cover. The image conjures the work of Giorgio Agamben and his revival of the ancient Roman concept of *homo sacer* or sacred man. In the final segment of this chapter, we turn to consider the relevance of Agamben's work for indigenous peoples, particularly as it relates to challenging the potentially crippling asymmetries of power that continue to define the tribal-federal political relationship.

THE INDIAN AS HOMO SACER

The Italian philosopher Giorgio Agamben revived the ancient Roman designation of *homo sacer* or "sacred man" to examine the exercise of exceptional sovereign power over an increasingly powerless subject, a life denuded of virtually all political rights and exposed to sovereign law as a "bare life." *Homo sacer* is a "juridical term from archaic Roman law designating an individual who, in response to a grave trespass, is cast out of the city. From the moment of his ritual pronouncement as a *homo sacer*, he can be killed with impunity by anyone but cannot be employed in sacrificial rituals that require the taking of a life. This 'sacred man' is thereby removed from the continuum of social activity and communal legislation; the only law that still applies to him is the one that irrevocably casts him out of the communal sphere."[99]

Agamben's interest, broadly speaking, is in interrogating what he calls the "inner solidarity between democracy and totalitarianism,"[100] where the "solidarity in question stems from a practice common in democratic and totalitarian forms of government: the appropriation of 'bare life' by the mechanisms of the state." Agamben's paradigmatic model for this interrogation is the concentration camp, a space in which "the most absolute conditio *inhumana* ever to appear on Earth was realized," where acts took place that "[exceed] the juridical concept of crime to such an extent that the specific political-juridical structure within which those events took place has often been left simply unexamined."[101] For Agamben, failing to interrogate carefully these specific political-juridical structures "obscures our view of the past," and "endangers our societies in the present."[102] Taken together, the idea of *homo sacer* and the bare life, the life denuded of virtually all political significance, represent for Agamben the *state of exception*, the condition wherein the rule of law is suspended indefinitely. Only the sovereign is empowered by the juridical order to declare a state of exception and in that moment, according to Agamben, the sovereign exists both inside and outside the juridical order (paradoxically, in mirror image to the *homo sacer*).[103] The sovereign's law exists by declaring itself inapplicable to certain persons or groups for an indefinite period of time. Agamben notes that "[h]e who has been banned is not, in fact, simply set outside the law and made indifferent to it but rather *abandoned* by it, that is, exposed and threatened on the threshold in which life and law, outside and inside, become indistinguishable. It is literally not possible to say whether the one who has been banned is outside or inside the juridical order" (emphasis in original).[104] As Mark Rifkin observes, "the generation of 'bare life' makes thinkable the consignment of those who do not fit the idealized 'biopolitical body' to a 'zone' outside of political participation and the regular working of the law but still within the ambit of state power." Those so designated "can be managed as 'bare life', as mere biological beings bereft of any/all of the legal protections of citizenship."[105]

Agamben's use of the term *homo sacer* may appear puzzling or ambiguous in light of the conventional translation of the concept as "sacred man." But he relies on an older, alternate meaning of *sacer*, one meaning cursed or taboo, as in the following definition of *homo sacer* derived from the Latin: "*Sacer* designates the person or the thing that one cannot touch without dirtying oneself or without dirtying; hence the double meaning of 'sacred' or 'accursed'."[106] Agamben notes that ancient Germanic and Scandinavian law contained a figure who was "brother to *homo sacer*," the *wargus* or wolf-man, an accursed character banished from the community. According to Agamben, "[t]he life of the bandit, like that of the sacred man, is not a piece of animal nature without any relation to law and the city. It is, rather, a threshold of indistinction and of passage between animal and man, *physis* and *nomos*, exclusion and inclusion: the life of the bandit is the life of the *loup garou*, the werewolf, who is precisely *neither man nor beast*, and who dwells paradoxically within both while belonging to neither."[107]

Like the *homo sacer*, the Indian nations have long subsisted in a liminal state within the Court's Indian law jurisprudence, dating back to their designation as "domestic dependent nations." They are entities *within* yet not *of* the body politic of the United States. Their powers of self-government preceded the formation of the US Constitution and are thus not subject to the Constitution's particularized constraints. Yet, paradoxically, tribes remain "subject to the dominant authority of congress, and their powers of local self-government are also operated upon and restrained by the general provisions of the constitution of the United States."[108] Their designation by the state as inferior savages, as a helpless and defenseless people, makes possible their consignment to a unique and totalizing form of sovereign power, held within the grip of federal plenary power, but rarely able to call upon the limiting or protective elements of law as other citizens. This impels us to interrogate closely and carefully the political-juridical structures that gave rise to and sustained this condition for Indian tribes through the modern era. It also impels us to question the legitimacy and morality of legal pronouncements that issue from the state and purport to constrain the acts of a sovereign that is both pre- and extra-constitutional. Finally, it impels us to inquire into and challenge the normative force that stereotypical, racist, and/or baseless conceptions of Indian people may continue to exert in the formulation and application of contemporary federal Indian law. As but one example, Indian people have been linked to the brother of *homo sacer* from early Germanic sources, the *wargus* or wolf-man, as revealed in this 1783 letter from George Washington to James Duane in which he articulates the underlying rationale for an Indian policy under the Continental Congress:

> I am clear in my opinion, that policy and oeconomy point very strongly to the expediency of being upon good terms with the Indians, and the propriety of purchasing their Lands in preference to attempting to drive them by force of arms out of their Country; which as we have already experienced is like driving the Wild Beasts of the Forest which will return as soon as the pursuit is at an end and fall perhaps on those that are left there; when the gradual extension of our Settlements will as certainly cause the Savage

> as the Wolf to retire; both being beasts of prey tho' they differ in shape. In a word there is nothing to be obtained by an Indian War but the Soil they live on and this can be had by purchase at less expence, and without that bloodshed, and those distresses which helpless Women and Children are made partakers of in all kids of disputes with them.[109]

There is one last element of Agamben's work that has particular resonance for this project and the status of Indian people and tribes within the United States. Agamben distinguishes between *constituting power* and *constituted power* and their relation to what he calls the *autonomy of potentiality*, and ultimately, to sovereignty. Constituted powers, according to Agamben, exist only *in* the state; they are "inseparable from a preestablished constitutional order, [and] need the State frame, whose reality they manifest. Constituting power, on the other hand, is situated *outside* the State; it owes nothing to the State, it exists without it, it is the spring whose current no use can ever exhaust" (emphasis in original).[110] In other words, constituting power is that "revolutionary and anarchic force" that leads to the creation of a new state; constituted power is the state's "conditioned and controlled form" that allows the state to exist in "its stabilized and, ideally, durable form."[111] Marking the elusive point of transition from the constituting to the constituted power of the state is difficult work but that is what a constitution is designed to do, to effectuate "the defusing and domesticating of precisely this 'constituting power', and the transformation of it into measures and guidelines for the exercise of a legitimate and properly legitimated 'constituted power'."[112]

For Agamben, following on Aristotle, understanding the relation between constituting and constituted powers is akin to understanding the relation between the *act* and the *autonomy of potentiality to act*. The architect retains his ability to design even when he is not engaged in the act of designing. The potentiality to act is autonomous from the act and, in order to preserve its distinct existence, must be that which does not transition into actuality. In Agamben's words, "This potentiality maintains itself in relation to actuality in the form of its suspension; it *is capable* of the act in not realizing it, it is sovereignly capable of its own im-potentiality."[113]

Leland de la Durantaye offers this helpful analysis of Agamben's autonomy of potentiality concept:

> When Aristotle speaks of the architect's potential to design buildings even in moments when he is not designing, and of the kithara player's potential for playing even when he or she is not playing, this is a potentiality independent of (or autonomous from) its actualization that presents no problems of understanding. When we acknowledge an individual's potential for doing this or that thing, we do not ask that he or she do it without interruption. If what he or she does is not exercised for too long, we may consider its continued existence questionable or vitiated. If the kithara player ceases to play for many years, we may have reservations about whether he or she can still play with anything like his or her former skill. But the idea of such autonomy is easily grasped (we must decide only about the half-life of various acquired skills). Thus, this potential could be said to be autonomous because in these instances it is independent of its actualization. What Agamben is arguing is the same as concerns the sovereign exercise of political power: that the state or the sovereign retains this potential to suspend the rule of law even when not doing so, just as we might say that in the stabilized form of constituted power the state retains the potentiality for exercising its full power to suspend the rule of law.[114]

The sovereign's potential to suspend the rule of law and create the state of exception captures perfectly one of the most insidious elements in all of federal Indian law, the notion that tribal sovereignty is subject to "complete defeasance" by Congress. The Court's most explicit reference to this power is contained in the modern era opinion in *United States v. Wheeler* (1978) where the Court describes the nature of tribal sovereignty in relation to federal power in the following words:

> [O]ur cases recognize that the Indian tribes have not given up their full sovereignty. We have recently said: 'Indian tribes are unique aggregations possessing attributes of sovereignty over both their members and their territory ...' [They] are a good deal more than 'private, voluntary organizations.' The sovereignty that the Indian tribes retain is of a unique and limited character. *It exists only at the sufferance of Congress and is subject to complete defeasance. But until Congress acts, the tribes retain their existing sovereign powers.* In sum, Indian tribes still possess those aspects of sovereignty not withdrawn by treaty or statute, or by implication as a necessary result of their dependent status. (emphasis added; citations omitted)[115]

Ironically, the source for this potentially lethal legal rule may have been Associate Justice Thurgood Marshall, long regarded as a justice most favorably inclined to supporting tribal claims for self-government. In a private memo to his fellow justices, dated January 16, 1978, five days after oral arguments in the case, Justice Marshall stated the following: "What strikes me as peculiar about the relationship between the tribes and the federal government is the plenary nature of Congress' authority to act vis-à-vis the tribes. Unlike the states, whose sovereignty (and concomitant police power) is protected and recognized in the Constitution, *the tribes continue to possess any criminal jurisdiction at all wholly at the sufferance of the federal government* (absent limiting treaty language)" (emphasis added).[116] On March 1, 1978, when Justice Potter Stewart circulated the first draft of his opinion in the *Wheeler* case, he included Marshall's "sufferance of the federal government" notion and, for good measure, embellished it with the "subject to complete defeasance" language to provide one of the most comprehensive, and chilling, judicial statements about the nature of tribal sovereignty in relation to federal power.

In these passages, we can discern some of the elements that signify what Agamben expressed as the "inner solidarity between democracy and totalitarianism," functioning as "the appropriation of 'bare life' by the mechanisms of the state." In relation to Indian tribes, the state functions in the mode of the revolutionary and anarchic forces that characterize the constituting power of the dynamic and emerging state. In claiming a power to subject tribal sovereignty to complete defeasance, the state reveals its imperialist posture and aspirations and commits itself to a (re)colonialized relationship with Native peoples. The *Wheeler* court's inclusion of the tribes' dependency status in its restatement of tribal–federal political relations serves to reify the racist ideology of the allotment era of federal Indian policy. The status of dependency functions as a juridical mask for the racialized discourse that perpetually subordinates the position of Native peoples and inscribes federal plenary power into the architecture of our democratic system. The *Wheeler* court appears oblivious to, or unconcerned about, their role in grafting elements of totalitarianism into their federal Indian law jurisprudence by handing Congress a blank check, or as Robert Williams suggests, a loaded gun to empire at will in Indian country.[117]

Williams's reference to a "loaded gun" borrows from the opinion of Justice Robert Jackson in the World War II era case, *Korematsu v. United States* (1944)[118] in which he dissented from the majority's approval of the federal government's internment policies directed at Japanese-Americans. In Agamben's terms, Justice Jackson was less concerned about the military order creating a state of exception than he was about the Court constitutionalizing the power to declare such an order for all time. In Justice Jackson's words:

> A military order, however unconstitutional, is not apt to last longer than the military emergency. Even during that period a succeeding commander may revoke it all. But once a judicial opinion rationalizes such an order to show that it conforms to the Constitution, or rather rationalizes the Constitution to show that the Constitution sanctions such an order, the Court for all time has validated the principle of racial discrimination.... The principle then lies about like a loaded weapon ready for the hand of any authority that can bring forward a plausible claim of an urgent need. Every repetition imbeds that principle more deeply in our law and thinking and expands it to new purposes. All who observe the work of courts are familiar with what Judge Cardozo described as 'the tendency of a principle to expand itself to the limit of its logic.'[119]

A final irony to note in the Indian law context: federal legislation tied specifically to Indian tribes relies on a political, not a racial, classification scheme, a reflection of the unique legal status of Indian tribes under federal law and the government-to-government relationship between the federal government and citizens of quasi-sovereign political bodies. As a result, courts do not apply the heightened strict scrutiny analysis that typically applies to race-based classifications in law. Instead, they apply a rational-basis standard that is highly deferential to the legislature. In the Indian law context, as the Court instructed in *Morton v. Mancari* (1974), this means Indian-specific legislation will be upheld so long as it is "tied rationally to the fulfillment of Congress' unique obligations towards the Indians."[120] In practice, this analysis cuts both ways and has been used to uphold laws that benefit individual Indians (e.g., employment preference rules for Indians within the federal Indian service), as well as laws that create disadvantages for individual Indians (e.g., application of differential, and harsher, criminal law schemes for crimes committed in Indian country).[121] In the final analysis, the *Mancari* standard preserves immense discretionary authority for the federal power to determine the substantive content of its "unique obligations towards the Indians."[122] In that sense, it functions as a weak source of legal protection, or *negative right*, for tribes to be free of federal policies that operate in invasive or destructive ways in relation to tribal rights of self-government. It functions even less perceptibly (or even not at all) as a source for affirmative claims, or *positive right*s, for tribes to be able to demand a greater share of resources from the federal government in support of their rights of self-government.

This extended analysis of the guardian-ward relationship between tribes and the federal government reveals the tribes' positional vulnerability within our democratic framework. Tribal sovereignty persists, to be sure, but the national commitment to ensure its continued expression and relevance remains fragile and tenuous. Treaty rights continue to have force unless and until a court determines that Congress has acted to abrogate the promises contained therein. Moreover, the Court has provided Congress with enormously broad latitude to legislate in Indian affairs. The thin reed of protection supplied by *Mancari* offers at least a colorable argument that legislation affecting tribes, as a political group must not disadvantage their political integrity or position. But in the modern era at least, the political branches have been the least of the tribes' concerns. The damage to the political and territorial integrity of tribes has come primarily from the Supreme Court in rulings that have led to the divestiture of large swaths of inherent tribal powers and a concomitant increase in the role that state law is permitted to have in Indian country. The Court's evolving use of concepts like *incorporation* and *dependency* has resulted in an ever-constricting conception of tribal sovereignty. Congress has acted, sparingly and cautiously, to recalibrate the flow of political power in tribal communities and thus far, has managed not to provoke a constitutional confrontation with the Court, though individual justices have been roused to issue caution signs alerting Congress "this far, and no further." The next chapter will explore the nature of these caution signs to assess the limits of Congress's power to reverse the tide of divestiture and redirect the trajectory of tribal sovereign authority to a more respectful, secure, and pluralist sphere. We will thus transition from this extended analysis of the ideological challenges that stand in the way of a more robust expression of tribal sovereignty and consider whether and how constitutional values and commitments may function in a similarly constraining way.

CHAPTER 5

Structure and Relationship: The Constitutional Dimensions of Federal and Tribal Power in Indian Country

When structure fails, liberty is always in peril.

Associate Justice Anthony Kennedy,
Public Citizen v. Department of Justice, 491 U.S. 440, 468 (1990)

In the previous chapter, we considered the modern Court's reliance on imperialist concepts like *incorporation* and *dependency* that led the Court to adopt an increasingly narrow theory of inherent tribal sovereignty. But this is not the entire story behind the modern Court's guarded approach to tribal powers. The emergent international concern with human rights in the post–World War II era and the legacy of the civil rights movement in the 1960s and 1970s have also influenced the modern Court's understanding of limits on *all* governments—federal, state, and tribal—when their laws unduly entrench upon individual rights and freedoms. As noted earlier, Indian tribes are not subject to the constraints of the US Constitution in their exercise of inherent tribal powers, although Congress has imposed most of the express provisions of the Bill of Rights onto tribal governments through the 1968 Indian Civil Rights Act. These statutory protections of individual rights and freedoms have not, however, fully assuaged the concerns of the modern Court, which has, on a number of occasions, expressed skepticism about the capacity and/or willingness of tribal governments and their courts to protect such fundamental individual interests. As Justice Anthony Kennedy noted in his opinion for the majority in *Duro v. Reina* (1990), "the tribes are left with broad freedom not enjoyed by any other governmental authority in this country. This is all the more reason to reject an extension of tribal authority over those who have not given the consent of the governed that provides a fundamental basis for power within our constitutional system."[1]

In the modern era, the constitutional challenge for policy makers, lawmakers, and academics is to articulate a vision for tribal sovereignty that avoids the imperialist impulses of past eras while ensuring that national commitments to liberal democracy and individual freedoms are duly honored and respected by tribal governments. This chapter will consider this important challenge in more detail.

In April 2012, the US Senate enacted legislation that presents this particular constitutional challenge in high relief. In its reauthorization of the Violence Against Women Act (VAWA) of 2012,[2] the Senate included language that would partially repeal the Court's decision in *Oliphant v. Suquamish Indian Tribe* (1978) and allow Indian tribes to prosecute *all* offenders, *including non-Indians*, who have significant and particularized ties to the prosecuting tribe and commit crimes in the narrowly prescribed areas of domestic and dating violence. The Senate's legislation was in direct response to the epidemic of violence against Native American women discussed in earlier chapters. The House of Representatives also enacted companion legislation to reauthorize VAWA but omitted the provisions that would recognize and affirm an enlarged scope of inherent tribal sovereignty in the enumerated areas, in part, because of concerns about the constitutionality of such measures. According to the House Report,

> Indian tribes are not foreign nations but rather 'domestic dependent nations' within the United States. Indian tribes are not parties to the U.S. Constitution and derive neither powers nor obligations from it. Tribes are therefore not subject to the government limitations enumerated in the Constitution, either directly via the Bill of Rights or through the Incorporation Clause of the 14th Amendment. The Supreme Court, in *Oliphant v. Suquamish Indian Tribe* (435 U.S. 191 (1978)), held the tribes do not have inherent sovereignty to try non-Indians. *It is an unsettled question of constitutional law whether Congress has the authority under the Indian Commerce Clause to recognize inherent tribal sovereignty over non-Indians.*" (emphasis added)[3]

The resulting political clash between the Senate and House versions of this legislation attracted considerable attention in the media[4] and stoked an intense debate among legal scholars, practitioners, and tribal advocates as to whether the expansion of tribal powers in this context was both justifiable and constitutional. Among those who entered the fray were fifty American law professors, including some of the most notable experts in federal Indian law, who submitted a joint letter to congressional leaders in late April 2012 expressing their "full confidence in the constitutionality of the legislation."[5] The law professors' letter relied principally upon the majority opinion in *United States v. Lara* (2004),[6] which upheld, largely on the basis of Congress's plenary power in Indian affairs, an amendment to the Indian Civil Rights Act of 1968 recognizing and affirming the tribes' inherent criminal jurisdiction over non-member Indians. The legislation upheld in

Lara effectively overruled the result in *Duro v. Reina* (1990),[7] which had applied and extended *Oliphant*'s implicit divestiture rule to deprive tribes of authority to prosecute nonmember Indian offenders. Beyond the authority of *United States v. Lara*, the law professors also noted that the VAWA reauthorization provisions imposed additional legal safeguards for offenders facing domestic and dating violence charges in tribal court that accorded them all rights guaranteed under the US Constitution. The Section of Individual Rights and Responsibilities of the American Bar Association issued a report in August 2012 that echoed the analysis and conclusion of the law professors.[8] In particular, the ABA Section leaders called attention to a provision of the VAWA legislation that requires tribes to provide "all other rights whose protection is necessary under the Constitution of the United States in order for Congress to recognize and affirm the inherent powers of the participating tribe to exercise special domestic violence criminal jurisdiction over the defendant."

Reaching the opposite conclusion, the Congressional Research Service (CRS) issued a report in April 2012 that expressed serious doubts about Congress's constitutional authority to relax the current restrictions on tribal criminal authority over non-Indians.[9] Regarding the VAWA provision noted above, the CRS report pointed to ambiguity in the report of the Senate Committee on the Judiciary about the nature and scope of rights that tribal courts were bound to provide if they elected to exercise this jurisdictional authority.[10] On one interpretation, tribes would have to provide the full panoply of constitutional rights guaranteed in state criminal prosecutions; on another reading, tribes would only have to guarantee the full range of statutory protections afforded under the Indian Civil Rights Act of 1968[11] and the Tribal Law and Order Act of 2010.[12] The difference, according to the CRS report, is that the former set of rights (derived from the Constitution) includes the right to trial by "a jury of one's peers and the right to counsel in misdemeanor cases where the defendant faces actual imprisonment."[13]

Without clarity on the precise nature of rights to be accorded to offenders in tribal court, the CRS report expressed doubts that current members of the Supreme Court would vote to uphold this law. This is particularly true in the case of Associate Justice Anthony Kennedy who concurred with the judgment in *United States v. Lara* but remained highly skeptical about Congress's power to subject US citizens to tribunals (like Indian tribal courts) that do not provide the full panoply of constitutional protections. The CRS report notes that of the five justices who supported the majority opinion in *Lara*, only Justices Breyer and Ginsburg remain on the Court today. Giving close attention to Justice Kennedy's concurring opinion in *Lara*, the CRS report concluded, "It is not clear that the Court considering a tribal court conviction under these bills would find that Congress has authority to expand the inherent sovereignty of tribes to try non-Indian defendants."[14] Given the apparent influence of Justice Kennedy's *Lara* opinion on the authors of the CRS report and his celebrated status as the "swing vote" on the Court, it behooves us to pay close attention to what this justice has been saying about congressional power in Indian affairs and the protection of individual liberty and freedom. As we will see, Justice Kennedy's jurisprudence has much to tell us about how the modern Court may approach the constitutional challenge described above as it relates to recalibrating the nature and scope of inherent tribal power.

Among contemporary justices of the Supreme Court, Justice Anthony Kennedy has been the most vocal in articulating constitutional limits on the federal power in Indian affairs, particularly if that power purports to enlarge or augment the scope of inherent tribal powers. The basis for Justice Kennedy's critique is a mode of constitutional interpretation known as *structuralism*. A basic definition for this approach works as follows: "As a method of interpretation, structuralism believes that the meaning of individual constitutional provisions can only be discerned by a thorough examination of the entire Constitution. Thus '[s]tructural arguments are inferences from the existence of constitutional structures and the relationships which the Constitution ordains among these structures'."[15]

Justice Kennedy has long employed a constitutional structuralist approach in his judicial opinions, including his majority opinion for the Court in *Duro v. Reina* (1990) and his concurring opinion in *United States v. Lara* (2004), as we will see further below. In general, Justice Kennedy's analysis has led him to find structural constraints on Congress's power to recognize and affirm a more robust expression of inherent tribal sovereignty. We will examine Justice Kennedy's structuralist approach in closer detail to determine if, in fact, it may take us in a different direction and enable us to find constraints on Congress's and the Supreme Court's power to deny or diminish inherent tribal powers. A positive answer to this query could help redirect the trajectory of tribal–federal relations in a direction that advances, instead of suppresses, the formative ethos of legal pluralism.

In his classic study, *Structure and Relationship in Constitutional Law* (the inspiration for the title of this chapter), Charles L. Black, Jr. sums up his preference for a structuralist, as opposed to a textualist, approach to constitutional interpretation in these succinct words: "[I]t is simply that the textual method, in some cases, forces us to blur the focus and talk evasively, while the structural method frees us to talk sense."[16] The structuralist approach closely resembles, in terms of methodology and aspiration, the search for what Laurence Tribe calls the "invisible Constitution" in a book of the same title.[17] Indeed, Tribe explicitly acknowledges his debt to Black for inspiring his project.[18] Tribe's objective is "to make 'visible' the Constitution's partial invisibility by setting before the reader the important respects in which the Constitution's commands, principles, and modes of operation and evolution go well beyond the words it contains."[19] These principles include the notion of popular sovereignty, the principles of judicial review, privacy and legality, and the commitment to non-secession of states from the union.[20] As with the structuralist approach, these principles are discerned by reasoning from the Constitution's structure and system of relations, with the caveat that "we cannot find in the invisible Constitution anything and everything we might wish."[21]

Black's analysis reveals the structuralist approach to be particularly well suited to resolving disputes that implicate separation of powers or federalism questions. As he demonstrates, however, resolution of broader questions of institutional and/or governmental structural arrangements often sheds light upon or directly impacts an individual's rights and his/her relationship with the state and federal governments. To illustrate, Black discusses the case of *Carrington v. Rash* (1965).[22] Carrington, a career army man stationed in El Paso, Texas, was denied the right to vote based on a state constitutional provision that allowed active military personnel to vote only in the county in which he or she resided at the time of enlistment. As an Alabama native when he enlisted, Carrington was precluded from ever rebutting the presumption of non-residency no matter how long he resided in Texas. The Supreme Court ruled for Carrington on the basis of the Fourteenth Amendment's Equal Protection Clause. As Black's analysis shows, however, that textual provision did not readily supply the answer to this constitutional problem. The Court duly noted the wide berth states normally have in setting the qualifications for voting, with the normative requirement that such qualifications be "reasonable." Texas was concerned that the voting rights of the local citizenry might be overwhelmed by large numbers of military personnel stationed in their county. The Court majority rejected Texas's proffered justification; the state's irrebuttable presumption of non-residency for military personnel violated Carrington's rights of equal protection.

Black's preferred mode of analysis for this case would have emphasized the constraints imposed upon the state emanating from the Constitution's structure and from Carrington's relationship with the federal government as a federal soldier. "Carrington," says Black, "was a federal soldier, recruited by the national government to perform a crucial national function." Texas's denial of voting rights is "the imposition, by a state, of a distinctive disadvantage based solely on membership in the Army. My thought would be that it ought to be held that no state may annex any disadvantage simply and solely to the performance of a federal duty."[23]

Black recognizes the limitations of a structuralist mode of constitutional interpretation, especially in situations where the dispute requires more precision, but he asks, "what 'test' purporting to rely on the commerce clause as text, and on an inference from it which is certainly formally invalid, has ever produced problems of less difficulty?"[24] He favors the structuralist approach, or as he says the "method of reasoning from structure and relation," because "to succeed it has to make sense—current, practical sense." The textualist approach can be "made to make sense, by legitimate enough devices of interpretation. But it contains within itself no guarantee that it will make sense, for a court may always present itself or even see itself as being bound by the stated intent, however nonsensical, of somebody else."[25]

Justice Kennedy draws from the same wellspring as Black in finding the structuralist approach to be an appealing and useful mode for constitutional interpretation, especially in cases relating to the distribution of governmental power (e.g., separation of powers, federalism) and their corollary impacts on the interest he prizes above all, personal and political liberty. As Frank Colucci notes in his fine biography of Justice Kennedy, "Kennedy recasts questions of government structure to implicate moral dimensions of personal and political liberty in order to defend a judicial role in enforcing boundaries of power. Social, economic, and political changes during the twentieth century make this judicial task difficult, he concedes. But courts still have an obligation to do what they can to restore the dignity of states and prevent the concentration of power in one branch or level of government."[26] For Kennedy, respecting the boundaries or spheres of power in our constitutional system of divided authority is essential for the preservation of freedom and liberty of the people. He embraces federalism, not "merely out of 'reverence for the Framers' or to preserve 'a faint vestige of our once proud diversity', but rather, because it "preserves an 'underlying, essential, ethical, moral value': that it is wrong, legally wrong, morally wrong, for a person to delegate authority over his or her own life to an entity which is so far removed from his or her ability to control it that he or she parts with the essential freedom that inheres in every human personality."[27] Kennedy subscribes to what Alison LaCroix calls the "constitutional law story" of federalism, conceiving of it as a radically new form of political organization that emerged from the 1780s efforts of the founders to draft and ultimately ratify the Constitution.[28] This may explain his penchant for frequently invoking the "genius of the Framers" in "split[ting] the atom of sovereignty" to challenge the Eurocentric view of an indivisible sovereign authority and to create a political system wherein individual freedom and liberty is secured by two governments, each acting within their appropriate spheres of authority, with the judiciary positioned to police the proper workings of political power.[29]

Justice Kennedy's structuralist approach traces a direct line of ideological authority to the framers in support of his analysis, as he demonstrated in a concurring opinion in *Clinton v. New York* (1998).[30] In voting to strike down the line-item veto, Kennedy called attention to Federalist 47 and its analysis for the horizontal distribution of political power within the federal government. For Kennedy, "the separation of powers doctrine 'was designed to implement a fundamental insight: concentration of power in the hands of a single branch is a threat to liberty'. Government structure protects individual liberty just as much as—if not more than—the 'freedom from intrusive government acts' included in the Bill of Rights."[31] On occasion, however, Justice Kennedy misspeaks in ascribing to the framers concerns or fears that are actually his own projected upon their words. Frank Colucci notes, for example, that Justice Kennedy advances a view of limited federal power rooted not only in the constitutional structure of enumerated powers but also in a conception of state power and sovereignty that is inconsistent with the framers' perspectives and concerns. According to Colucci, "Publius feared that the states would threaten liberty and stability by interfering with and encroaching upon the rightful powers of the federal government. Kennedy uses Publius' language to support his fear that the greatest threat to liberty arises not from the states but from congressional and federal overreach. Kennedy's motivations actually invert the assumptions and fears of Madison."[32]

Justice Kennedy has employed his favored structuralist approach in some of his Indian law opinions, at times in subtle moves and at other times, as the centerpiece of his analysis. We will examine three opinions, all arising in the context of challenges to the scope of the tribe's inherent sovereign authority to prosecute offenders for violations of tribal criminal law. The imperative for paying such close attention to Justice Kennedy's views on this subject, and for understanding his methodological approach in resolving the legal issues, is twofold. First, Kennedy is one of the few contemporary justices who have attempted to articulate a principled framework for understanding political relations among tribes, the states, and the federal government, and the limits of their respective powers in relation to US citizens. Second, as he does in so many other areas of law, Justice Kennedy often holds the swing vote on matters relating to inherent tribal powers and more generally, on federal authority in Indian affairs. To be sure, the traditional ideological alliances among conservative and liberal members of the Court often do not hold true in the Court's federal Indian law cases. Nonetheless, Justice Kennedy's ideological and methodological approach in these cases has the strong potential to capture a majority of the Court if Congress were to pass legislation that affirms or recognizes a greater scope of inherent tribal sovereign authority. Indeed, this is precisely the situation described above with regard to the proposed federal legislation reauthorizing the Violence Against Women Act, and its partial repeal of the *Oliphant* decision in the context of domestic and dating violence involving Native women. According to former Senator Daniel Akaka, then-Chairman of the US Senate Committee on Indian Affairs and a sponsor of the draft legislation, the bill "recognizes and strengthens concurrent tribal criminal jurisdiction to investigate, prosecute, convict, and sentence both Indians and non-Indians who assault Indian spouses, intimate partners, or dating partners, or who violate protection orders, in Indian country."[33] Justice Kennedy's extant views on the limits of federal power to recognize and affirm a greater measure of inherent tribal sovereign powers are thus quite significant and have the potential to tilt the arc of Supreme Court opinion in the direction of or away from the formative ethos of legal pluralism.

The first case we will consider is *Oliphant v. Schlie* (1976), a decision from the US Court of Appeals for the Ninth Circuit.[34] Justice Kennedy dissented from the panel decision that ruled in favor of the Suquamish Indian Tribe and affirmed the tribe's inherent sovereign authority to prosecute a non-Indian (Mark Oliphant) for violating tribal criminal law. As we know, the US Supreme Court reversed the decision of the court of appeals in *Oliphant v. Suquamish Indian Tribe* (1978).[35]

It is hard to imagine a fact pattern better suited to appeal to Justice Kennedy's concern for personal and political liberty; a non-Indian American citizen living on tribal reservation lands faced criminal charges from a tribal sovereign government in which he had neither formal representation nor avenues for membership or political participation. In the aftermath of the Court of Appeals' decision in favor of the tribe, Mark Oliphant told the media, "The Constitution of the United States ... doesn't apply in this town. It's a punch in the nose is what it is."[36] Washington state Attorney General Slade Gorton sounded a similar theme in his criticism of the Ninth Circuit's decision: "What it does is to disenfranchise American citizens." Oliphant's attorney, Phillip Malone, was more blunt in his indictment of the Ninth Circuit's opinion: "It's Hitler."[37]

Although Justice Kennedy's dissenting opinion in *Oliphant v. Schlie* does not directly implicate the Constitution (and rightly so, since *Talton v. Mayes* (1896)[38] held that the Constitution does not constrain the inherent powers of tribal sovereign authority), it embraces "invisible" constitutional principles or values like popular sovereignty in conceiving of tribal sovereignty as not including authority over non-Indians. For Kennedy, tribal sovereignty is a malleable juridical concept that functions in different ways depending upon whether the central issue is resolving structural conflicts over the distribution of political power among the tribes, state, and federal governments or testing the limits or reach of inherent tribal sovereign authority. In the former instance, tribal sovereignty helps to test the reach of state law into Indian country in light of federal policies that accord a measure of autonomy for Indian tribes. In that setting, Kennedy says that tribal sovereignty functions merely as a "veil" over what is essentially a question of federal preemption in the field of Indian affairs. This explains why he parted company with the majority and resisted importing the broad view of tribal sovereignty derived from *Worcester v. Georgia* (1832); for Kennedy, that decision is properly understood as a case responding "to a state's attempted invasion of tribal privileges that had express federal sanction." In short, the broad notion that inherent tribal sovereignty presumptively exists unless Congress has expressly declared otherwise, the rule the majority derived from the *Cherokee Nation* cases, is simply inapplicable in cases challenging the scope or limits of inherent tribal sovereign authority. In those cases, the concept of tribal sovereignty functions differently. It serves to describe the tribal interest in maintaining its cultural identity or its self-governing status. But for Kennedy, it lacks any independent dispositive value in determining the scope of tribal power. That determination turns on the extent to which federal policy supports the purported expression of tribal power or as Kennedy says, is "consistent with the powers granted by Congress to tribal governments during the past 100 years."

Kennedy relies expressly on the allotment-era imperialist formulation of federal plenary power in Indian affairs to assert, without qualification, "the power of Congress to divest tribes of *any and all* of their sovereign attributes is, of course, undisputed" (emphasis added). Citing the recent congressional acts terminating the *sovereign* existence of several Indian tribes (Kennedy's actual statement inadvertently reads in a decidedly more genocidal tone—"legislation has terminated the existence of various Indian tribes"), Kennedy reifies the Court's declaration from *United States v. Kagama* (1886) and states anew that "only two truly sovereign entities exist at any place within the geographical limits of the United States: the federal government and the states of the union."

Kennedy's narrow conception of sovereignty, coupled with his focus on the cultural distinctiveness of Indian tribes, provides an additional argument against tribal criminal authority over non-Indians. Mirroring the concerns of the Court from another nineteenth-century precedent, *Ex Parte Crow Dog* (1883)[39] about the morality of trying Indian offenders in accordance with "white men's standards of justice," Kennedy expressed deep concern about subjecting a white man to "cultural standards to which he is not accustomed." Kennedy's concerns on this point ring hollow, especially considering that the tribal charges against Mark Oliphant hardly implicated distinctive tribal cultural values; he was charged with assaulting a tribal police officer and resisting arrest. Oliphant spoke truthfully when he said, "it's a punch in the nose, is what it is."

In the final analysis, Kennedy was guided by his understanding of tribal and federal juridical relations from the past century and their apparent accommodation on how to address reservation-based crimes. More importantly, Kennedy's views endorse the nineteenth-century imperialist view of federal power that structures tribal authority in a position wholly subordinate to and dependent upon Congress and limits the scope of tribal power to managing political relations among their members. For Kennedy, tribal authority over non-Indians is inconsistent with that broader history; "[v]iewing tribal courts in their historical and cultural context, in light of the fact that virtually no white man appears to have been tried by an Indian tribunal in the past century, congressional silence on this point can be hardly be viewed as assent."

In the second opinion under consideration, *Duro v. Reina* (1990),[40] Justice Kennedy authored the Court's majority opinion in finding that Indian tribes lacked the inherent sovereign authority to prosecute non-member Indian offenders who violated tribal criminal laws. While Kennedy's opinion again relies on the allotment-era imperialist formulation of federal power in Indian affairs, it also embraces the concerns of modern liberal democracy in regard to individual liberty and freedom. To that extent, the opinion provides important guidance on how the modern Court seeks to mediate tribal sovereignty claims in light of those broader national commitments. Kennedy's majority opinion is noteworthy for imposing the Western-derived theory of *consent of the governed* to limit the reach of inherent criminal tribal powers to tribal members only and for locating structural constraints emanating from the Constitution on the power of Congress to subject American citizens to criminal proceedings before tribunals not subject to the full panoply of constitutional protections for individuals.

Deriving its ideological footing from the *Oliphant* and *Wheeler* opinions, Kennedy's opinion first notes that Indian tribes, as a consequence of being subject to the overriding authority of the United States, no longer possess full territorial sovereignty or the authority to enforce their laws against all who come within their juridical spaces. Instead, their retained sovereignty is limited to "that needed to control their own internal relations, and to preserve their own unique customs and social order." Tribal prosecution of political outsiders, a manifestation of attempting to manage external relations, is inconsistent with their dependent status and could only occur "by delegation from Congress, subject to the constraints of the Constitution." While Kennedy acknowledges that Indian tribes, in many instances, retain a broader measure of civil and regulatory authority over *all* persons within their territories, their authority in the criminal realm is necessarily constrained, since it represents "a far more direct intrusion on personal liberties." The defendant's status as a non-member of the tribe precluded him from participating in the political life of the tribe, including denying him the right to vote, hold office or to serve on a jury. In essence, since he shared with Mark Oliphant the perpetual status of political outsider to the tribe, the tribe was subject to the same juridical limitations as in the *Oliphant* decision.

Structure and relationship come to the fore in Justice Kennedy's opinion when he outlines why Indian tribes retain the inherent sovereign authority to prosecute their own tribal members (the holding of the Court in *United States v. Wheeler*) despite their status as US citizens and thus, presumptive beneficiaries of the government's purported solicitude to protect them against "unwarranted intrusions on their personal liberty." The tribes' inherent sovereign authority to prosecute their own members comes "from the consent of its members, and so in the criminal sphere membership marks the bounds of tribal authority." Tribal citizenship also helps overcome the Court's concern about US citizens who are also tribal members being exposed to *peculiarized* tribal juridical systems. While the Court acknowledges that tribal legal systems share common features with the dominant American systems, tribal court systems are nonetheless "influenced by the unique customs, languages, and usages of the tribes they serve. Tribal courts are often 'subordinate to the political branches of tribal governments', and their legal methods may depend on 'unspoken practices and norms.'" Most significantly, tribal courts are not subject to the constraints of the Constitution and the protections of the Bill of Rights. The Indian Civil Rights Act of 1968 offers what the Court terms "statutory guarantees of fair procedure," but as Kennedy quickly notes, these are "not equivalent to their constitutional counterparts," as exemplified by the absence of a right to appointed counsel for indigent offenders.

Moving further than he did in his dissenting opinion in *Oliphant v. Schlie*, Justice Kennedy uses both textual constitutional protections (e.g., right to appointed counsel) and structural guarantees of liberty embedded within the *invisible constitution* (e.g., separation of powers, independent judiciary, judicial proceedings governed by the principle of legality, the principle of democratic accountability) to highlight both the fundamental differences in the structural and ideological operations of tribal judicial systems and implicitly, their normative deficiencies in comparison to the dominant American systems. Presumably, the tribal members' consent to being citizens of the tribe and their capacity, at least theoretically, to affect the nature and quality of the tribe's political infrastructure in general, and its judicial systems in particular, are sufficiently compelling factors for the Court to tolerate this expression of illiberal governance within the American constitutional system. To the extent this represents a nod to legal pluralism, it is certainly a weak expression of it since the Court's limited deference to inherent tribal power functions mainly to mark its judicial tolerance for normatively distinctive cultural societies imposing their rules upon members only. The Court employs the familiar nineteenth-century doctrine of incorporation and the veil of US citizenship to constrain the territorial and personal reach of tribal law. Tribal criminal authority over non-member Indians, on the other hand, represented a far greater threat to liberal democracy's superstructure. As an expression of legal pluralism, such tribal authority stretched beyond the Court's tolerance for illiberal systems operating within the nation's constitutional framework.

The final element of the Court's analysis that bears on structure and relationship is its reference to structural constitutional limits on the power of Congress to alter these arrangements, particularly in the direction of augmenting the scope of tribal powers over non-members. According to Justice Kennedy, "[o]ur cases suggest constitutional limitations even on the ability of Congress to subject American citizens to criminal proceedings before a tribunal that does not provide constitutional protection as a matter of right." The case cited in support of this proposition is *Reid v. Covert* (1957), a decision precluding Congress from subjecting civilian dependents of military personnel to court-martial in military tribunals outside the continental United States that did not accord the full panoply of constitutional protections.[41] The Court's opinion in *Reid*, as in *Duro v. Reina*, noted both constitutional textual (e.g., no right to trial by jury or provisions for grand jury indictment) and structural limitations (e.g., conflation of powers exercised by the Executive Branch) on Congress's power to authorize such actions. The *Reid* court was particularly concerned that Congress had apparently authorized the Executive branch to develop the substantive and procedural rules of decision governing in the military tribunals. Such a role represented the conflation of legislative, executive, and judicial functions within one branch of government. According to the Court, "[s]uch blending of functions in one branch of the Government is the objectionable thing which the draftsmen of the Constitution endeavored to prevent by providing for the separation of governmental powers."[42]

The *Duro* court again distinguished the situation of tribal members whose consent provided the necessary additional authority for this extraordinary exercise of sovereign authority. According to the Court, "tribes are left with broad freedom not enjoyed by any other governmental authority in this country." For Justice Kennedy, this was "all the more reason to reject an extension of tribal authority over those who have not given the consent of the governed that provides a fundamental basis for power within our constitutional system."

As noted earlier, the Court reveals no hesitation in assessing the normative legitimacy of tribal sovereign authority through the lens of Western political ideology. Even here, the Court applied the consent of the governed principle in more stringent form than it does in other areas of federal Indian law or within the dominant legal system, a point noted by the dissent in *Duro*. Justice Brennan's dissent highlighted the fact that the Court's precedents had not required consent of the governed in order to uphold tribal civil jurisdiction over non-members. Nor had the Court required consent of the governed before the state or federal governments could prosecute nonresidents or aliens, respectively, neither of whom were eligible to participate in the political life of the polity.

In related fashion, the Court's reference to *Reid v. Covert* seems quite inapposite, since military tribunals, unlike tribal governments, derive their authority from delegated federal authority and are thus within the orbit of constitutional constraint, at least as they relate to US citizens. Nonetheless, the reference was a classic Kennedy move to call attention to the possible constraints emanating from the Constitution's structure that would prohibit Congress from enacting sweeping legislation to subject non-members and their liberty interests to criminal trials before tribal courts. For Kennedy, it seemed vitally important to recognize the judiciary's role in policing the structural boundaries of federal and tribal power to ensure that the personal and political liberty of non-members was not unnecessarily compromised. Recalling his words from *Clinton v. New York* (1998), Kennedy stated, "the Framers of the Constitution could not command statesmanship. They could simply provide structures from which it might emerge."[43]

Justice Kennedy's analytical approach in *Duro v. Reina* was the subject of a fascinating private memorandum from Justice Antonin Scalia to Justice William Brennan, with a copy to Justice Thurgood Marshall, the two dissenters in *Duro*. Apparently, Justice Scalia had initially planned to join the dissent in the case. His memo to the other two justices explains his reasons for leaving them and joining the majority. It sheds light not only on Kennedy's approach in the case but also on the Court's analytical approach to its Indian law cases generally. In relevant part, Justice Scalia wrote the following:

> My initial reaction to the case was based on my certainty that when the arrangements governing Indians were established in the 19th century ... the inhabitants of Indian territory were regarded as consisting of two classes, Indians and non-Indians—and that there would have been no thought of providing for an Indian from another tribe to be treated like a non-Indian for tribal jurisdictional purposes. I am still persuaded of that, but efforts to craft an opinion have also persuaded me of the reality that our opinions in this field have not posited an original state of affairs that can subsequently be altered only by explicit legislation, but *have rather sought to discern what the current state of affairs ought to be by taking into account all legislation, and the congressional 'expectations' that it reflects,*

> *down to the present day.* I would not have taken that approach as an initial matter, but it seems too deeply imbedded in our jurisprudence to be changed at this stage. And if one takes that approach, I think Tony has the better of the argument." (emphasis added)[44]

Justice Scalia's memorandum confirms an earlier observation that the Court seems preoccupied with vindicating the interests of non-members of Indian tribes and their views that they never expected to be subjected to tribal jurisdiction. Justice Kennedy's opinion for the Court hues to that line of reasoning, and reinforces it with the structural limitations critique in an attempt to preclude future congressional action that would alter the status quo in the tribes' favor.

Of course, Congress did respond to the *Duro* decision in remarkably short order, in large part due to well-organized lobbying by tribal leaders and their supporters.[45] Beyond the ideological and structural concerns of the opinion, *Duro* also triggered a rash of practical problems for tribes, notably a jurisdictional void in criminal law enforcement in Indian country where conceivably no sovereign would have the authority to prosecute non-member Indian offenders. In response, Congress amended the Indian Civil Rights Act in 1991 to declare that "the inherent power of an Indian tribe, hereby recognized and affirmed, [includes the power] to exercise criminal jurisdiction over all Indians."[46] The question of whether Congress possessed the constitutional authority to enact such a law came before the Court in *United States v. Lara* (2004).[47] Justice Kennedy's concurring opinion in *Lara* is the third and final opinion that we will consider in assessing his structuralist approach to constitutional interpretation.

The Court's majority opinion in *United States v. Lara* (2004), authored by Justice Stephen Breyer, held that Congress has the "constitutional power to lift the restrictions on the tribes' criminal jurisdiction over nonmember Indians" as its amendment to the Indian Civil Rights Act sought to do. While the focus of our analysis is on Justice Kennedy's concurring opinion, we must note a couple of salient points about the Court's majority opinion before moving on. First, the Court declares that the Constitution grants to Congress "broad general powers to legislate in respect to Indian tribes, powers that we have consistently described as 'plenary and exclusive.'" The majority anchors this extraordinarily broad authority in the Constitution's Indian Commerce Clause and the Treaty Clause. Citing an earlier precedent from 1989, the Court notes that the "central function of the Indian Commerce Clause" is to "provide Congress with plenary power to legislate in the field of Indian affairs." That passage is remarkable and disturbing for its profound misreading of the Court's own jurisprudential history. As our earlier analysis revealed, the Court's recognition of federal plenary power in Indian affairs arose during the late nineteenth century, at the height of a new wave of US imperialist activity both at home and abroad. Indeed, the Court's decision in *United States v. Kagama* (1886) expressly rejected the federal government's reliance on the Indian Commerce Clause as support for the Major Crimes Act of 1885. Instead, the Court upheld the law on the basis of a racialized, dependency theory rooted in the so-called guardian–ward relationship between the federal government and Indian tribes. Repeated iterations of the government's self-proclaimed plenary power in Indian affairs became more commonplace in the twentieth century but even through the early 1980s, the Court's Indian law cases continued to reflect ambiguity as to the precise source of this massive federal authority. In *McClanahan v. Arizona Tax Commission* (1973), the Court admitted that the "source of federal authority over Indian matters has been the subject of some confusion, but it is now generally recognized that the power derives from federal responsibility for regulating commerce with Indian tribes and for treaty making."[48] Less than a decade later, in *Merrion v. Jicarilla Apache Tribe* (1982), the Court renewed the confusion by citing to the Constitution's text and to the non-textually based, dependency theory as the source of federal power in Indian affairs: "When Congress acts with respect to the Indian tribes, it generally does so pursuant to its authority under the Indian Commerce Clause, *or by virtue of its superior position over the tribes*" (emphasis added).[49] In 1989, the Court inexplicably conflated the two distinct sources of federal power, ostensibly so that Congress's virtually unchecked, imperialist power in Indian affairs would have some measure of constitutional pedigree. Thus, in *Cotton Petroleum Corporation v. New Mexico* (1989), the Court pronounced that the "central function of the Indian Commerce Clause is to provide Congress with plenary power to legislate in the field of Indian affairs."[50] The *Lara* court's nonreflective citation to *Cotton Petroleum* drew a sharp response from Justice Clarence Thomas who chided the Court for its failure to find a textually based constitutional provision supporting Congress's power to alter the scope of tribal sovereignty.

The second aspect of *Lara*'s majority opinion worth noting is the Court's unprecedented reference to an additional source of federal power in Indian affairs, one that even pre-dates the formation of the Constitution (and thus, is *pre-constitutional*). According to the Court, US–Indian relations during most of the first century of the new nation's existence operated largely in accordance with the norms of military and foreign relations. In that light, "Congress' legislative authority would rest in part, not upon 'affirmative grants of the Constitution', but upon the Constitution's adoption of preconstitutional powers necessarily inherent in any Federal Government, namely, powers that this Court has described as 'necessary concomitants of nationality'."[51] While it is entirely unclear what the Court actually portends by this new formulation of federal power in Indian affairs, the implications for tribes are worrisome. The Court's approach cannot be described as structuralist, since it references a preconstitutional regime of relations with no connection to the set of formative values and norms that were embedded, either explicitly or implicitly, within the Constitution. Moreover, the reference to Indian affairs as an aspect of military and foreign policy obscures the strong tradition and policy of bilateralism, whereby the European, and later, the American, governments engaged in treaty-based relations with Indian tribes in recognition of each other's sovereignty to ensure peaceful coexistence between Indian and non-Indian societies. The Court's reference to this preconstitutional history of early American–Indian relations effectively transforms what was largely a regime of bilateralism into an ahistorical nationalistic license to rule in a unilateral and imperialist fashion. This form of self-aggrandizing decision-making was, unfortunately, quite characteristic of the Court's Indian law jurisprudence from the late nineteenth and early twentieth centuries. It is unsettling, to say the least, to see the Court reify some of its most unsavory juridical practices from the past in the contemporary setting. As Frank Pommersheim cautions, this preconstitutional source of federal power, conjoined with the *Kagama-Lone Wolf* extraconstitutional source of federal power, means that "federal authority in Indian law is to be found above and below, outside and under, but *not in* the Constitution."[52]

Justice Kennedy issued a concurring opinion in which he agreed that the majority properly rejected *Lara*'s double jeopardy argument. Congress's amendment of the Indian Civil Rights Act restored tribal criminal jurisdiction over non-member Indians (like Lara) by relying on the concept of inherent, not delegated, tribal sovereign authority. Lara's sequential prosecutions by tribal and federal authorities arising from the same events were therefore not violative of the Constitution, since the prosecutions were by separate and distinct sovereigns. For Kennedy, that finding was sufficient to dispose of the case. He parted company with the majority in its formulation of a broader holding for the case, that is, that the Constitution authorizes Congress to allow Indian tribes, pursuant to their inherent sovereignty, to prosecute non-member Indians. Justice Kennedy notes that this holding is "on a point of major significance to our understanding and interpretation of the Constitution; and, in my respectful view, it is most doubtful."

Kennedy initially reiterates the Court's historical view that inherent tribal powers were largely operative upon the tribe's own members. He then quickly moves into the most detailed and robust structuralist analysis of federal power in Indian affairs that he has authored to date. Despite its length, it is worth reciting the core of Justice Kennedy's structuralist analysis in full, with only citations or parenthetical expressions omitted:

> Lara, after all, is a citizen of the United States. To hold that Congress can subject him, within our domestic borders, to a sovereignty outside the basic structure of the Constitution is a serious step. The Constitution is based on a theory of original, and continuing, consent of the governed. Their consent depends on the understanding that the Constitution has established the federal structure, which grants the citizen the protection of two governments, the Nation and the State. Each sovereign must respect the proper sphere of the other, for the citizen has rights and duties as to both. Here, contrary to this design, the National Government seeks to subject a citizen to the criminal jurisdiction of a third entity to be tried for conduct occurring wholly within the

territorial borders of the Nation and one of the States. This is unprecedented. There is a historical exception for Indian tribes, but only to the limited extent that a member of a tribe consents to be subjected to the jurisdiction of his own tribe. The majority today reaches beyond that limited exception.

The Court resolves, or perhaps avoids, the basic question of the power of the Government to yield authority inside the domestic borders over citizens to a third sovereign by using the euphemistic formulation that in amending the ICRA Congress merely relaxed restrictions on the tribes. There is no language in the statute, or the legislative history, that justifies this unusual phrase, and, in my respectful view, it obscures what is actually at stake in this case. The terms of the statute are best understood as a grant or cession from Congress to the tribes, and it should not be doubted that what Congress has attempted to do is subject American citizens to the authority of an extraconstitutional sovereign to which they had not previously been subject. The relaxing-restrictions formulation is further belied by the involvement of the United States in all aspects of the tribal prosecution of a nonmember Indian. Federal law defines the separate tribes, the broader class of "Indians," the maximum penalty which the tribes may impose for crimes, and the procedural protections to which defendants are entitled in the trials. This does not indicate the sort of detachment from the exercise of prosecutorial authority implicit in the description of Congress' act as having relaxed restrictions.

In addition to trying to evade the important structural question by relying on the verbal formula of relaxation, the Court also tries to bolster its position by noting that due process and equal protection claims are still reserved. That is true, but it ignores the elementary principle that the Constitutional structure was in place before the Fifth and Fourteenth Amendments were adopted. To demean the constitutional structure and the consent upon which it rests by implying they are wholly dependent for their vindication on the Due Process and Equal Protection Clauses is a further, unreasoned holding of serious import. The political freedom guaranteed to citizens by the federal structure is a liberty both distinct from and every bit as important as those freedoms guaranteed by the Bill of Rights. The individual citizen has an enforceable right to those structural guarantees of liberty, a right which the majority ignores. Perhaps the Court's holding could be justified by an argument that by enrolling in one tribe Lara consented to the criminal jurisdiction of other tribes, but the Court does not mention the point. And, in all events, we should be cautious about adopting that fiction.

The present case, however, does not require us to address these difficult questions of constitutional dimension. Congress made it clear that its intent was to recognize and affirm tribal authority to try Indian nonmembers as inherent in tribal status. The proper occasion to test the legitimacy of the tribe's authority, that is, whether Congress had the power to do what it sought to do, was in the first, tribal proceeding. There, however, Lara made no objection to the tribe's authority to try him. In the second, federal proceeding, because the express rationale for the tribe's authority to try Lara—whether legitimate or not—was inherent sovereignty, not delegated federal power, there can be no double jeopardy violation. For that reason, I concur in the judgment.[53]

Justice Kennedy's concurring opinion in *Lara* serves as an exemplar of his structuralist approach to constitutional interpretation, and most particularly, his strategy of recasting "questions of constitutional structure in the rhetoric of personal liberty, implicating the same moral considerations as matters of individual rights."[54] From Kennedy's perspective, the fundamental question about the power of Congress to subject US citizens to an extraconstitutional sovereign is properly left for another day, but he leaves no doubt about his views on the matter. For Kennedy, the structural guarantees of personal and political liberty are as fully enforceable against the federal government as the textually based freedoms embodied in the Bill of Rights. Therefore, even if Congress were inclined to affirm a broader scope of inherent tribal sovereignty to include authority over non-members, Kennedy locates constraints on that federal power emanating from the constitutional structure and the distinct protections of individual liberty flowing there from.

The flaws in Kennedy's structuralist approach are twofold. First, while he locates structural limits on Congress's power to affirm a *broader* scope of inherent tribal powers, he has never identified similar structural limits on the power of Congress to *diminish or eliminate* such tribal powers. During the course of Justice Kennedy's tenure on the Supreme Court, he has shown no indication that he has moved away from the views he expressed in *Oliphant v. Schlie*, when, as a member of the federal appeals court, he described the substantive federal power in Indian affairs as follows: "The power of Congress to divest tribes of *any and all of their sovereign attributes* is, of course, undisputed" (emphasis added).[55] Indeed, Justice Kennedy has consistently taken the view that Congress has wide latitude to empire at will within Indian country, a view that also envisions a diminished and wholly subordinated political position for Indian tribal governments in relation to federal (and state) governments.

The second flaw in Kennedy's structuralist approach in *Lara* is its implicit endorsement of a federal prerogative to interfere with and/or invade the internal political processes of another sovereign entity, here, the Indian tribes, in order to advance federal objectives or policies. In his criticism of the *Lara* majority's "relaxing-restrictions formulation," Justice Kennedy highlights the heavy hand of the federal government that is necessarily implicated in tribal prosecutions of non-member Indians, including federal laws that "define the separate tribes, the broader class of 'Indians', the maximum penalty which the tribes may impose for crimes, and the procedural protections to which defendants are entitled in the trials." For Kennedy, "[t]his does not indicate the sort of detachment from the exercise of prosecutorial authority implicit in the description of Congress' Act as having relaxed restrictions."

When the targets of such invasive federal action were the states, Justice Kennedy and his fellow justices did not hesitate to hold the federal power in check, as in *Alden v. Maine* (1999).[56] In his opinion for the majority, Kennedy cited both textually based and structurally based constitutional limitations on Congress's power to subject states to private lawsuits within their own courts. The Court noted that such action would actually be more offensive to the dignity of state sovereignty than a federal law subjecting states to private suits in federal court. As Justice Kennedy explained for the Court, "[a] power to press a State's own courts into federal service to coerce the other branches of the State, furthermore, is the power first to turn the State against itself and ultimately to commandeer the entire political machinery of the State against its will and at the behest of individuals. Such plenary federal control of state governmental processes denigrates the separate sovereignty of the States."[57] He added further, "When the Federal Government asserts authority over a State's most fundamental political processes, it strikes at the heart of the political accountability so essential to our liberty and republican form of government."[58]

Tribal governments are, as a general matter, not afforded similar protection against such invasive federal action. The principle reason for that differential treatment is the Court's view that tribal sovereignty is simply qualitatively different from, and inferior to, the sovereign integrity of the several states of the union. In the hands of the Court, the concept of tribal sovereignty has been treated as juridical play dough, a malleable substance that can be shaped and formed, augmented or diminished, at the will of the federal sovereign. In over two hundred years since the ratification of the Constitution, the Supreme Court has yet to formulate an authoritative, principled and legitimate rationale to justify this unbridled form of national power. In his concurring opinion in the *Lara* case, Justice Clarence Thomas finally gave voice to this reality. He wrote, "The court utterly fails to find any provision of the Constitution that gives Congress enumerated power to alter tribal sovereignty. The Court cites the Indian Commerce Clause and the treaty power. I cannot agree that the Indian Commerce Clause 'provide[s] Congress with plenary power to legislate in the field of Indian affairs'. At one time, the implausibility of this assertion at least troubled the Court, and I would be willing to revisit the question" (citations omitted).[59] For Justice Thomas, "[i]t is quite arguably the essence of sovereignty not to exist merely at the whim of an external government."[60] The treaty power, as Justice Thomas correctly surmises, is equally inapposite as it confers power on the executive branch, not the legislative branch, to "make Treaties." Asserting otherwise is particularly ironic, according to Justice Thomas, in light of Congress's Act in 1871 unilaterally ending treaty making with Indian tribes, an Act that Thomas regards as "constitutionally suspect."[61]

The central problem, as Justice Thomas observes, is that "federal Indian law is at odds with itself."[62] The Court's late nineteenth- and early twentieth-century Indian law jurisprudence represents both the nadir of tribal sovereignty and the zenith of federal plenary power. This historical period coincided with a wave of US imperialism at home and abroad and a resurgence of American nationalism that operated aggressively and systematically, often through force of law, to choke off expressions of sociocultural diversity that deviated too far from the template of an agrarian, Anglo-Saxon, Christian nation-state. In the modern era, the political branches of the federal government have often attempted to recapture the formative ethos of legal pluralism by engaging with Indian tribes in a spirit of political partnership and sovereign cooperation. Unfortunately, these efforts have been severely crippled by the Court's insinuation of the most regressive elements of its Indian law jurisprudence, features that reify historically racialized views of Indian tribes and Indian people as deficient, deviant societies with untenable claims to the exercise of political power over anyone but their own membership.

This is the reason Justice Kennedy's structuralist approach will continue to yield unfavorable results from the perspective of Indian tribes. While he regularly employs the rhetoric of liberal democracy and its associated concerns with individual liberty and freedom, Kennedy seems unable to resist resorting to imperialist-era conceptions of tribal governmental systems and their relative inferiority to the national power. In other words, Kennedy's juridical aperture setting is affixed to the plenary power era of federal–Indian relations, an angle of vision that effectively excludes the light from either the formative era of federal–Indian relations or the modern era of tribal self-determination. A wider aperture setting would take in the whole complexity of federal–Indian relations, including the legacy of treaty-making before 1871, when political relations were characterized by negotiated bilateral agreements between tribes and the federal government. To be sure, we must acknowledge the historical reality that even in the era of bilateralism, deals with Indian tribes were often made "with the price in one hand and the sword in the other."[63] In that light, a wider aperture setting would actually sharpen our ability to discern and critique the Court's use of the virulent forms of legal fictions like *incorporation* and *dependency* in ways that revive and entrench the experience of colonialism for Indian people.

A broader and more inclusive historical perspective would inform the structuralist approach to constitutional interpretation and advance a proper understanding of the scope of federal power in Indian affairs. The approach would open the space for including the perspectives and the expectations of tribal societies and make it feasible to envision a regime of shared governance on commonly occupied territories. It would take in the modern era of tribal self-determination in which federal, tribal, and state political actors work actively and cooperatively with each other, mindful of but not shackled to the history of colonialism, to develop workable and complementary systems of tribal governance that address the vital needs of their communities while also respecting the normative values and interests of the broader federal polity. What Justice Kennedy wrote about federal–state relations applies with equal moral force to federal–tribal relations: "Although the Constitution grants broad powers to Congress, our federalism requires that Congress treat the States in a manner consistent with their status as residuary sovereigns and joint participants in the governance of the Nation."[64]

In short, a *revised and inclusive* structuralist approach offers the potential to challenge, reassess, and even reject the major premises underlying the field of federal Indian law. These major premises—an unfettered federal plenary power in Indian affairs, a tribal sovereignty subject to complete defeasance, and limitations imposed on the scope of inherent tribal power calibrated by conformity to a status of domestic dependent nationhood—are inevitably and hopelessly mired in the muck of colonialism. They serve as regressive, crippling agents to the project of tribal self-determination and force contemporary political actors to work within an atavistic parallel universe where blatant racism and profound levels of distrust and disrespect taint the preponderant attitude toward Native peoples.

The revised and inclusive structuralist approach to constitutional interpretation, finally, enables us to articulate a new way of situating Native rights within the paradigm of legal pluralism, the idea that multiple legal systems can actually coexist peacefully within shared territories. It allows Native peoples to confront the tyranny of "monism"—the Western-derived idea that there can only be ONE source of legitimate authority, ONE God, ONE sovereign, ONE nation, and ONE national memory. Of course, this ideological reformation of tribal-federal relations will entail substantial re-envisioning and redesign of an institutional apparatus better suited to advance, and not suppress, the ethos of legal pluralism. We turn to consider this subject in the final chapter.

CHAPTER 6

Coming Full Circle: (Re)Building Institutions to Advance the Ethos of Legal Pluralism

During Senate confirmation hearings in 1994, Senator Larry Pressler (R-SD) asked Supreme Court nominee Judge Stephen Breyer for his opinion on whether non-Indian residents of Indian country ought to have recourse to the federal courts, after exhausting their remedies in tribal courts, to vindicate claims under the Indian Civil Rights Act. Judge Breyer responded, "Well, my substantive instinct is, of course, that if the procedures and protections in the tribal court can be brought to match those in the Federal court, the problem will tend to go away, because then, of course, you would have the same protection in both places. And that is not a judicial question. That is a question of people meeting and understanding and talking to each other and trying to work out appropriate procedures."[1]

The impetus for Senator Pressler's question was the politician's equivalent of the liberalist and constitutional challenges described earlier, that is, determining the proper measure of autonomy that ought to be accorded to tribal sovereigns while also respecting our national commitments to liberal democracy and individual freedom. In the early 1980s, Senator Pressler (and others) introduced legislation that would have partially repealed the Supreme Court's decision in *Santa Clara Pueblo v. Martinez* (1978) and allowed any individual, after exhausting their remedies in tribal court, to seek federal court review of alleged violations of their rights under the Indian Civil Rights Act.[2]

In response to Senator Pressler's query, Judge Breyer suggested an answer that relied less on judicially produced results than on negotiated institutional arrangements between tribal and federal governmental leaders that sought to achieve some comparable level of rights protection in both regimes. Breyer's observation implicitly acknowledges the limitations of the judicial process in mediating these sorts of questions. Litigated matters, of necessity, are intensely fact-contingent and law-bound and rarely lend themselves to the production of holistic or comprehensive remedies. Negotiated institutional arrangements in the context of intergovernmental disputes, on the other hand, offer opportunities for more carefully calibrated solutions that address the myriad, and often clashing, interests on the respective sides. They may also include procedural protections that take into account the imbalances of power that may exist among the negotiating entities. This is a critical factor in the context of tribal–federal relations, since tribal governments are perennially at risk of having to be the entities to suppress or compromise particularized interests in order to accommodate the federal interests. For tribes, the challenge is to preserve as much of the distinctive cultural and social elements that relate to the communal and individual sense of identity as indigenous peoples while being responsive to the demands and commitments of the overarching and dominant federal polity. As Frank Pommersheim has cautioned, tribal legal systems must not be corralled into mimicking majoritarian legal systems; otherwise, "the work of colonization and assimilation is complete."[3] The aim, therefore, is to craft institutional arrangements or, to borrow Duncan Ivison's concept—pursue an *institutional design approach*—to encourage constant and open dialogue between tribal and federal systems of government about matters of shared interest and concern. Ivison's institutional design approach seeks to

> create a 'circulation of power between authorities, rather than allowing its systematic unequal accumulation'. So instead of authority and jurisdiction always being a matter of belonging to either the state or the group, the institutional design approach accepts the multiplicity of possible jurisdictional lines and the need for coordination and interaction between them. Neither the group nor the state should ever acquire a monopoly of control over a contested social arena that 'affects individuals both as group members and citizens' (the 'no-monopoly restraint'). And finally, members and citizens must be provided with clear options which enable them to actually choose between these different jurisdictions, up to and including opting out of the relevant jurisdictions and choosing another.[4]

In this final chapter, we will examine some of the prominent legal and political institutional arrangements that have been or might be employed to mediate the varied, and sometimes conflicting, interests of the tribal and national/state polities that make up our constitutional democracy. Each of these proffered arrangements—enhanced statutory protections, constitutional amendments, revival of treaty-making, and conventions on tribal sovereignty—will be assessed in light of their potential to redirect the trajectory of tribal–federal relations in the direction that best reflects the ethos of legal pluralism.

ENHANCED FEDERAL STATUTORY PROTECTIONS FOR TRIBAL SELF-GOVERNMENT

Since 1975, with passage of the Indian Self-Determination and Education Assistance Act,[5] Congress has enacted a plethora of statutes to advance the self-determining aspirations of tribal nations in areas relating to self-government, education, health care, economic development, environmental and natural resource protection, land claims, repatriation of ancestral remains and items of cultural patrimony, and protection of sites possessing sacred qualities.[6] Some of these laws operate in the form of devolution of authority from the national government to tribal communities, while others establish a regime of intergovernmental co-management where tribal governments work cooperatively with either state or federal polities on specified subject areas. Tribal compacting with the federal government for local control of education or health care systems is an example of the former arrangements, while the tribal–state compacting regulatory framework to operate reservation-based casinos under the Indian Gaming Regulatory Act of 1988[7] is an example of the latter.

Recent scholarship has criticized the latter arrangements as a form of modern-day encroachment on tribal sovereignty that creates an environment of *forced federalism* wherein tribes are compelled to "negotiate with state governments for policy jurisdiction regarding governance, taxation, economic development, hunting and fishing on Native homelands, and so on."[8] Other scholars take the view that such forms of intergovernmental dialogue and shared responsibility are the inevitable result of living in a tripartite sovereign polity, where no single sovereign has (or ought to have) the luxury or prerogative to act in isolation from the others. As Frank Pommersheim notes, "Tribal communities must also realize that dialogue and negotiation with the state on legitimate issues is not a 'sell-out' of tribal sovereignty but simply part of the contemporary political and legal struggle to achieve a tribal sovereignty that advances the flourishing of tribal life."[9]

While these recent federal statutory and policy developments unquestionably have made positive impacts in Indian country, they represent profoundly limited advances in the overarching project of empowering tribal governments and advancing tribal self-determination. First, they rely on the political goodwill of federal lawmakers who ultimately must be able to support these initiatives at the stage of their conceptualization and at the time of voting on appropriations. Second, and quite related to the first point, these statutory and policy developments inevitably serve to further entrench the primacy and dominance of federal control and power in the lives of tribal communities. Federal–tribal relations currently function within a *theater of benevolence*, where the efforts to accommodate and secure tribal political autonomy take place within the poles of federal support and concern, on the one hand, and federal paternalism and dominance, on the other. Within this regime, tribal sovereignty is performed under a critical imperialist gaze and is subject to unilateral revision by the dominant sovereign. In short, the federal aspiration to channel federal power in ways that are supportive, not destructive, of tribal powers remains a challenge in the modern era. President Richard Nixon, in his 1970 Message to Congress on Indian Affairs, summed up the federal aspiration and challenge in this way:

> This, then, must be the goal of any new national policy toward the Indian people: to strengthen the Indian's sense of autonomy without threatening his sense of community. We must assure the Indian that he can assume control of his own life without being

> separated involuntarily from the tribal group. And we must make it clear that Indians can become independent of Federal control without being cut off from Federal concern and Federal support. It is a new and balanced relationship between the United States government and the first Americans that is at the heart of our approach to Indian problems.[10]

Finally, notwithstanding their positive impacts in Indian country, these recent federal statutory and policy developments have rarely served to redress or overcome the hemorrhaging of inherent powers of tribal sovereignty precipitated by contemporary decisions of the US Supreme Court. Earlier, we highlighted one exception to this pattern where Congress acted quickly in response to the Court's decision in *Duro v. Reina* (1990) to acknowledge and affirm tribal inherent power to prosecute non-member Indians for violations of tribal criminal law.

As detailed in the previous chapter, Congress may provide an additional exception to this pattern if it ultimately enacts legislation that would partially repeal the *Oliphant* decision and restore tribal sovereign authority over all offenders, *including non-Indians,* in prescribed cases of domestic and dating violence. This initiative would build on legislation from 2010 when Congress enacted the Tribal Law and Order Act that, among other things, authorized Indian tribes to sentence offenders up to three years for any one offense and allows consecutive sentences up to a maximum of nine years.[11] The so-called enhanced tribal court sentencing authority is contingent on a tribe providing licensed counsel to indigent defenders in a judicial setting presided over by a licensed and law trained judge in accordance with published and accessible substantive and procedural tribal criminal laws.

The proposed legislation and the already-enacted Tribal Law and Order Act of 2010 represent real, substantive progress in the effort to build greater capacity in Indian communities to deal with what the US Senate has called "an epidemic of domestic violence and sexual assault" in Indian country.[12] But at the end of the day, these sorts of subject-specific, piecemeal approaches to enhancing tribal sovereign powers present an unduly cumbersome challenge for tribes who are often required to develop particularized regulatory and/or adjudicatory structures that are principally designed to meet federally imposed requirements and conditions as opposed to tribally determined needs. More importantly, these laws increasingly signal to Indian tribes that the price tag for enhanced sovereign authority is a form of *juridical assimilation,* where the operative systems and substantive protections of the dominant sovereign are imposed on tribal governments in a process that may be ostensibly consultative but hardly dialogic. Additionally, these unilateral approaches often fail to recognize or address the institutional and structural deficits (e.g., gaps in educational achievement and vocational training, disparities in personal and community health, pervasive alcohol and chemical dependencies, generational impairments to traditional and spiritual practices and belief systems, telecommunications and transportation networks, among others) that serve as perennial obstacles to effective tribal self-governance. Troy A. Eid, the chair of the Indian Law and Order Commission, an advisory body authorized by the Tribal Law and Order Act of 2010 to recommend additional reforms in federal Indian policy, acknowledged as much when he stated, "[M]any of the greatest challenges to securing equal justice for Native Americans living and working on Indian lands are structural. They're rooted in a system of federal institutions, laws and practices that pre-date the modern era of tribal sovereignty and self-determination, and which [the Tribal Law and Order Act] does little or nothing to change."[13] According to Eid, the Indian Law and Order Commission is charged with "looking beyond the horizon" in formulating recommendations to the federal government. Among the subjects the Commission will examine is the juvenile justice system for Native American offenders. Native Americans make up approximately two-thirds of the entire population held in the federal juvenile justice system, a result of federal legislation tied specifically to crimes committed by Indian offenders in Indian country. The widespread confinement of young Native Americans in federal institutions, like the earlier state practices of involuntary removal of Indian children from their families, poses obvious challenges for tribal communities hoping to perpetuate their culture and to transmit traditional values to the next generation of tribal members.

In sum, continued reliance on federal legislation as the driver of institutional reforms in the federal–tribal relationship does very little to alter the verticalized, imperialist political relationships between these sovereigns. The federal government is positioned at the dominate end of the axis and ultimately determines the substantive content of the federal–tribal agenda and the level of accommodation it is prepared to make to tribal interests. This is the political equivalent of a *tribal sovereignty of sufferance* on the ground. While federal policy makers may consult with tribes on new initiatives (as exemplified by the proposed legislation that would partially repeal the *Oliphant* decision), the resulting product would hardly qualify as a bilaterally negotiated framework to advance tribal self-governance. As a consequence, the extant regime of enhanced federal statutory protections has little potential to redirect the trajectory of tribal–federal relations in a direction that best reflects the ethos of legal pluralism.

CONSTITUTIONAL AMENDMENT TO SECURE TRIBAL SOVEREIGNTY

Leading scholars in the field of federal Indian law, from Russell Lawrence Barsh and James Youngblood Henderson in the late 1970s and early 1980s to Frank Pommersheim in 2009, have proposed securing tribal sovereignty within the structure of the US Constitution.

In their path-marking book, *The Road: Indian Tribes and Political Liberty* (1980),[14] Barsh and Henderson suggest a constitutional amendment that, at its core, accords tribes the same constitutional status as states. The amendment purports to recognize a form of full territorial sovereignty for tribes so that their authority would extend over all persons within the tribe's territory, "concurrent only with the general Constitutional authority of the United States."[15] Unless expressly delegated to the United States, tribal powers are reserved and cannot be divested by Congress. The proposed amendment addresses tribal representation in the federal polity by the creation of two auxiliary chambers, a Tribal Senate Caucus and a Tribal House Caucus, whose representation would be equal in the former chamber (one delegate from each tribe), and proportional in the latter (one delegate for every five thousand tribal members). Two caucus members from each chamber would be named to serve in the "regular" US Senate and House of Representatives. Finally, the amendment prohibits the application of state law within tribal territories in the absence of a compact with tribes that is approved by Congress while it also disenfranchises tribal members residing in tribal territories, prohibiting them from voting in state elections.

Perhaps the most laudable element of the Barsh and Henderson proposed constitutional amendment is its explicit extinguishment of federal plenary power in Indian affairs and its restoration of full territorial sovereignty to tribal governments. Conceptually, however, it embraces the *incorporation*—as opposed to the *confederation*—model of inter-sovereign union and folds tribal sovereignty into the structural matrix of the federalist constitution. As a result, it exposes tribal legal systems to continued review and potential diminishment by the judiciary, whose authority to apply the entirety of the Constitution to tribal governments is left unchecked by this proposed amendment. Under this amendment, tribal theocracies like the Pueblos of the southwest could be deemed constitutionally suspect as violative of the Establishment Clause of the First Amendment. Denying the franchise in tribal elections to non-member reservation residents might also be deemed violative of constitutional guarantees of equality in voting. In short, the suggested amendment does not accept the concept of tribal sovereignty on its own terms, as an ideologically unique and distinct form of sociopolitical organization that cannot, and should not, be re-envisioned in the guise of Western statehood in order to be legitimized and protected. More fundamentally, the proposed amendment lacks the quintessential element underpinning the American constitutional state—the consent of the governed that legitimates the governing authority of the polity. Robert Clinton's critique of such constitutional amendments holds quite true in this case: "Since amendments are proposed by Congress, where the Indian tribes have no structural protections and virtually no effective representation, and are ratified by the states, not the tribes, any such constitutional amendment might be thought to resolve technical legal defects about the purported scope of federal authority under the Indian Commerce Clause, but cannot supply the consent of the Indian tribes required to bring the exercise of power over the Indians into conformity with America's basic commitments to constitutional delegation of authority by those governed."[16]

Frank Pommersheim suggests a much more succinct constitutional amendment in his book, *Broken Landscape: Indians, Indian Tribes, and the Constitution* (2009).[17] Pommersheim's proposed amendment states the following:

> The inherent sovereignty of Indian tribes within these United States shall not be infringed, except by powers expressly delegated to the United States by the Constitution.
>
> The Congress shall have power to enforce, by appropriate legislation, the provisions of this Article.[18]

As Pommersheim explains, his proposed amendment draws on other constitutional provisions, namely the Tenth and Fourteenth Amendments, in order to "provide respectful and durable constitutional recognition of inherent tribal sovereignty, which harks back to the original text of the Constitution, with a new sense of respect and inclusion."[19] Although Pommersheim asserts that a constitutional amendment is "the surest footing to advance and uphold tribal sovereignty in this newest of eras in Indian law,"[20] it is not entirely clear how his proposed amendment escapes the conceptual and ideological flaws observed in the Barsh and Henderson proposal. Specifically, it would appear that tribal powers would remain subject to diminishment or elimination by either the Congress or the Supreme Court, particularly following the Court's declaration in *United States v. Lara* (2004) that the central purpose of the Constitution's Indian Commerce Clause is to provide Congress with plenary power to legislate in Indian affairs. Furthermore, while Pommersheim underscores the critical importance of tribal consent as an element of any constitutive reform effort, it is not clear how his proposed amendment embraces tribal consent, either at the constitutional ratification stage or at the implementation stage. Like the Barsh and Henderson proposal, Pommersheim's suggested amendment opts for the incorporation model of union, as opposed to the confederated model, and thereby thrusts tribal sovereignty more deeply into the matrix of constitutional federalism. While this approach may well accord greater protection for the dignity and durability of tribal legal systems, the price it may exact for such protection could be the loss of truly distinctive sociocultural elements of indigeneity that would inevitably be chipped away or erased in order to "fit" tribal polities within the constitutive structures of Western governments. This would obviously undercut the move toward an institutional framework that best reflects the ethos of legal pluralism.

TREATY-BASED FEDERALISM

American Indian activists who led the Trail of Broken Treaties march to Washington in 1972 framed their demands against the federal government in a Twenty-Point plan, the first of which called for the "Restoration of Constitutional Treaty-Making Authority."[21] Since then, a number of legal scholars have echoed the demand for a revival, in some fashion, of bilateral practices in the management of tribal–federal relations.[22] Robert Clinton is among those scholars advocating a return to what he calls *treaty federalism*, "the bilateral negotiation of the tribal–federal relationship" as the conceptual model best suited to advance the project of tribal self-governance. For Clinton, "[s]uch mutual respect and recognition would go far to redress the legacy of colonialism and polish the chain of friendship which once bound the Indians to the United States and helped secure the very existence of the United States during the American Revolution."[23]

Frank Pommersheim is among the critics of the treaty federalism approach. Conceptually, according to Pommersheim, the fact of American citizenship for all American Indians makes a return to treaty-making quite untenable, since it raises the specter of a nation formulating treaties with a discrete subgroup of its own citizenry. This, of course, assumes that the federal government would even be willing to repeal its unilateral ban on treaty-making with Indian tribes dating back to 1871. Furthermore, there are the political realities that tribes have very little leverage to compel the federal government to come to the treaty-making table or to revise the extant jurisprudential landscape in a way that undercuts the government's superior political position in relation to Indian tribes. Finally, Pommersheim notes the practical difficulties of reaching agreements (and attaining Senate ratification) with the over 565 federally recognized Indian tribes currently operating distinct governments today.[24]

The conceptual advantage of the treaty federalism approach is that it more closely approximates the confederation model of political union, the regime that respects the autonomy and differently sourced sovereign authority of the compacting polities that occupy and govern within shared territories. It recalls the elements of trust, mutual dependence, and respect that characterized the formative arrangements between Indian tribes and Euro-American states in the formative era of Western–indigenous relations.[25] Moreover, it is the only extant constitutionally sanctioned mechanism by which the federal government is expressly empowered to conduct relations with Indian tribes.

But Pommersheim is right to call attention to the asymmetrical distribution of political power between the federal government and the tribes. Such an approach in the modern era would also have to contend with the reality that states have grown accustomed to a substantial role in reservation-based governance. Thus, any approach that excluded the states—formally or informally—would likely face stiff opposition. Finally, while the treaty-federalism approach implicitly assumes that neither polity possesses the capacity to terminate the sovereign existence of the other, there are no explicit or reliable structural mechanisms that would prohibit this from actually occurring. In short, federal plenary power would lurk as an omnipresent and anarchic *constituting power* (to borrow Agamben's phrase), in whose shadows tribal sovereigns would continue to operate. While tribal nations would have the force of morally and legally binding arrangements on their side as security for their rights to political and territorial integrity, it is uncertain whether they would be able to avoid a reprise of *Lone Wolf v. Hitchcock* (1903) where a reviewing court might set aside treaty arrangements in light of changed circumstances. Thus, the project of tilting the arc of tribal–federal relations to better reflect the ethos of legal pluralism would move quite tentatively, at best, under this approach.

CONVENTIONS ON TRIBAL SOVEREIGNTY

In my earlier work, *American Indians and the Law* (2008), I called for a return to bilateral arrangements between tribes and the federal government as the preferred vehicle to secure and advance tribal sovereignty in the modern era.[26] Borrowing from developments in international law, I suggested that these bilateral arrangements should operate under the rubric of *conventions on tribal sovereignty*. Unlike the tribe-specific treaty-making practices of the eighteenth and nineteenth centuries, conventions on tribal sovereignty would be expressed through a framework agreement or *master treaty* between tribes and the federal government. This mechanism expressly signals what is at stake here—a *belated exercise in state-building*—whereby the interests of distinct polities who share common territories are brought together within the matrix of a separate and distinct constitutive text that is not uniquely the province of either polity, and thus not shackled to one or the other's normative values, traditions, or aspirations.

There is a deeper, normative dimension to this conventions approach to tribal sovereignty that speaks to what should be at the core of any institutional or structural arrangements that may be produced by the federal and tribal nations. Here, we speak about the set of values and norms that animate and legitimate the institutional framework and give it, in Agamben's terms, *constituted* (as opposed to *constituting*) force. The noted philosopher James Tully has written eloquently and insightfully about constitutional conventions in the particular context of indigenous and Western peoples and argues for a system of intersocietal constitutional dialogue that is guided by conventions of *mutual recognition, continuity and consent*. According to Tully, "[c]onstitutional 'conventions' in this common-law sense are norms that come into being and come to be accepted as authoritative in the course of constitutional practice, including criticism and contestation of that practice. They gradually gain their authority by acts in conformity with them and by appeals to them by both sides, as warrants of justification, when they are transgressed."[27]

Without being too prescriptive about the actual mechanics of the process, the conventions approach contemplates representatives from the distinct polities developing the framework for political coexistence that is interest-focused, not polity focused. In other words, the driving moral force behind the formation of the conventions would be consensus on how best to advance shared interests, including personal and political liberty, equal protection and due process of the laws, and security for their respective ways of being and distinct world views. Conceptually, this approach embraces the *confederation model of political union*, as opposed to the *incorporation model*, and thus explicitly aims for the creation and operation of a structural framework for intergovernmental cooperation. Such a structuralist approach, like Ivison's *institutional design approach*, would create the requisite space for accommodating social and cultural differences while respecting shared political values about the limits of legitimate government. To borrow from Charles Black, the conventions approach frees us to "talk sense." If federal and state policy makers are concerned about the nature of legal protections afforded to individuals subject to tribal jurisdiction, for example, then these concerns can and should be addressed explicitly in this framework arrangement. Is an independent judiciary essential to the protection of individual rights? If so, are those rights structurally endangered if judges are selected through an electoral, as opposed to an appointment, process (as is the case in the majority of the states)? The conventions process, in short, would require each of the polities to assert and defend their normative political preferences, as well as the structural mechanisms that best advance and secure those preferences. Creating space for indigenous perspectives to be heard and debated on a level playing field would contribute to what Burke Hendrix calls "creative intellectual tension for surrounding settler populations, particularly if [indigenous peoples] are allowed greater space to put their social conceptions into political practice."[28]

The particular arrangements or institutions that may be produced through the conventions approach could conceivably take many forms. Tribal and federal leaders could, for example, initially establish a bicameral body—a *commission* or *house of delegates*—composed of representatives from each of the polities who serve prescribed terms and whose principal initial charge would be the crafting of a framework agreement or *master treaty* that would articulate the foundational principles for mutual recognition, continuity and consent. As Tully has noted, many of these foundational principles derive from centuries-long constitutional practices (in the common law sense) that have yielded norms now seen as authoritative. First and foremost among these foundational principles is the recognition of tribes as distinct sovereign bodies with powers of self-government. This is, and should continue to be, the lodestar principle at the core of the conventions approach. The principle of federal plenary power in Indian affairs, likewise, is the product of centuries-long constitutional practice, but unlike the norm of recognized tribal sovereignty, this norm is not viewed as authoritative—at least by advocates of tribal sovereignty—and certainly has functioned (and is capable of still functioning) contrary to the conventions of mutual recognition, continuity, and consent. There would therefore be a compelling argument for the bicameral body to reject explicitly the principle of federal plenary power in the framework agreement.

This is not to suggest that national commitments to liberal democracy and the primacy of individual freedoms would or should be compromised in any way through the conventions approach. As a matter of constitutional practice and tradition, tribal governments and institutions have long acknowledged the practical and ideological importance of demonstrating respect for individual rights and freedoms, whether grounded in traditional cultural norms or Western-derived rights.[29] As Frank Pommersheim notes, an important goal for tribal governments and institutions is "to produce a creative body of law that synthesizes the best of the dominant legal system with the legal imperatives of tribal history and culture, while at the same time avoiding dominant pressures that would render such a synthesis irrelevant or contrary to the national interest."[30] Interestingly, in its *Oliphant* opinion, the US Supreme Court expressed a similar view about the nature of tribal sovereign authority when it noted that "their exercise of separate power is constrained so as not to conflict with the interests of this overriding sovereignty."[31] Both perspectives anticipate the need for accommodation of the other's interests and values, though it is likely the *Oliphant* court did not envision this accommodation to be a shared or mutual obligation on the part of the federal government. Nonetheless, the bicameral body could fashion an *ethic of mutual accommodation* as a core principle of the framework agreement.

Earlier, we noted that Duncan Ivison's notion of an institutional design approach for state–group relations included what he termed *reversal points*, a sort of interest-protecting safety valve whereby "vulnerable members can seek a remedy from another jurisdiction in case of situations where threats to their basic rights or capabilities fail to be addressed."[32] Such reversal points already exist in contemporary federal Indian law through which individuals, in prescribed situations, may seek review and/or challenge a tribe's jurisdictional authority in federal court.[33] These reversal points are, however, *imposed* rather than *negotiated* (or in Ivison's terms, *discursively legitimated*) and would therefore be ripe for review and reconsideration by a bicameral body. To be clear, the existence of negotiated reversal points is a critically important aspect of this project and is vital to helping tribal governments enhance their reputation as justice-rendering political bodies. In its review, the bicameral body could recommend the alternative fora (e.g., federal courts, an intertribal court of appeals, or a newly created appellate body) to which an individual could apply for redress, prescribe the types of cases or issues that are appropriate for such an option, and articulate the nature of the review that such forums would be authorized to undertake.

Certain elements of the proposed framework arrangement would likely necessitate federal action, namely congressional legislation that would operationalize the normative orders, recommended systems, or procedures enumerated in the framework agreement. Such legislation could, for example, prescribe the rules of decision that would henceforth apply in federal courts in cases involving or implicating the interests of Indian tribes. As noted in earlier chapters, the common law rule of implicit divestiture has proven to be a lethal weapon in the hands of the modern Court, leading to the erasure of a substantial measure of inherent tribal power. The proposed framework agreement could influence the course of federal legislation in calling for an end to the use of this toxic theory. In this regard, the conventions approach would ensure a richer, more meaningful form of engagement between tribal and federal polities on issues that truly affect tribal self-determination on the ground in Indian country.

As described above, a framework agreement produced under the rubric of the conventions on tribal sovereignty approach has the potential of addressing both *individual claims* (including those that derive from an individual's status as a US citizen, as a tribal member, or some mix of the two) and *collective claims* implicating the sovereign interests of the tribal government and its institutions. The proposed federal legislation that would partially repeal the *Oliphant* decision and (re)affirm inherent tribal criminal jurisdiction over all offenders in domestic and dating violence cases is an exemplar of cases that have serious implications for both individual and collective claims. The legislation purports to recalibrate the nature and scope of inherent tribal power over US citizens who have no reasonable possibility of participating politically in the affairs of those sovereign bodies.

As the analysis in chapter 5 suggests, there is credible debate as to whether Congress has the constitutional authority unilaterally to enact such legislation. To be sure, there is no guarantee that federal legislation based on bilaterally negotiated terms developed through the proposed framework agreement under the conventions approach would fare better as a constitutional matter. After all, the Supreme Court has struck down provisions of voter-approved state constitutions as violative of the federal constitution.[34] Nonetheless, the conventions approach offers the possibility for the respective polities to reach consensus on the basic terms for protecting shared values like individual liberty and due process that would also meet the constitutional standards of the tribes and the federal government.

Likewise, in disputes between tribal members and their own tribes, the conventions approach offers the possibility of devising mutually agreed-upon mechanisms or institutions that address such individual claims while also respecting the tribe's collective sovereign interests. In recent years, tribal and federal courts have experienced a dramatic increase in claims by individual Indians who claim to have been wrongly disenrolled as members of their tribes. Federal courts are largely sympathetic to these claims but they almost universally reject the claims on jurisdictional grounds and/or on the basis of tribal sovereign immunity. In *Lewis v. Norton* (2005), for example, the Court of Appeals for the Ninth Circuit dismissed a disenrollment claim on sovereign immunity grounds but not before stating that it found the case "deeply troubling on the level of fundamental substantive justice."[35]

Perhaps the most widely known tribal enrollment dispute involves the Cherokee Nation and the Cherokee Freedmen whose ancestors, former slaves of the Cherokee Nation, were accorded tribal citizenship in an 1866 treaty with the United States following the Civil War. In 2007, the

Cherokee Nation amended its membership rules to require proof of blood lineage from a Cherokee ancestor, effectively disenfranchising those Freedmen who were unable to document such blood ties. While the Cherokee Nation leadership frames this issue as an exercise in tribal sovereignty, the Freedmen regard the tribe's action as an unlawful denial of basic tribal citizenship rights rooted in racism.[36] The dispute spilled over into both tribal and federal courts, and even into the halls of Congress where members of the congressional Black Caucus threatened to withhold federal appropriations to the Cherokee Nation unless it restored the citizenship rights of the Freedmen.[37] The resulting discourse brought together two complex and highly contentious national stories, the "complicated tangle" of race/racial identity politics and the legacy of colonialism.[38] Even allowing for the principle that a "tribe's right to define its own membership for tribal purposes has long been recognized as central to its existence as an independent political community,"[39] actions like that of the Cherokee Nation risk exposing their tribal institutions, and by extension, those of all tribal governments, to charges of illegitimacy in light of the disrespect shown for individual rights and freedoms. Such actions on the part of tribes complicate, and indeed endanger, any project urging a greater measure of autonomy for tribal nations. Taylor Keen, a former member of the Cherokee Nation Tribal Council, was among the few tribal leaders openly to support the claims of the Freedman. Shortly before the 2007 vote to amend the tribal constitution, he stated, "This is a sad chapter in Cherokee history. But this is not my Cherokee Nation. My Cherokee Nation is one that honors all parts of her past."[40]

In contrast to the actions of the Cherokee Nation, other tribal courts have demonstrated more concern and respect for individual rights in the context of membership disputes.

In *Snowden v. Saginaw Chippewa Indian Tribe*, for example, the tribal appellate court treated membership status in the manner of a vested right under the tribe's constitution, revocable in very limited instances and only after affording the member full rights of "due process and cultural respect."[41] The widespread attention that these intra-tribal disputes have garnered and the concomitant scrutiny of tribal systems that often results underscore the importance of developing mutually agreed-upon mechanisms or institutions that address such individual claims while also respecting the tribe's collective sovereign interests.[42] While the proposed framework agreement may not devolve to that level of detail, it could certainly provide the organizing principles and operational framework through which such issues could be redressed more effectively.

Finally, conventions on tribal sovereignty, as expressed through the proposed framework agreement, ought to be structured in a way that requires periodic review and renewal by its constituent polities. This element of review and renewal was a critical element of indigenous diplomatic relationship building in the colonial and early American period. As Robert Williams points out, "[r]enewal, in fact, was regarded as a continuing constitutional obligation of treaty partners."[43] Williams recalls the example of the eighteenth-century Creek tribal leader named Stumpee who explained the wisdom and necessity of constitutional renewal to Georgia's colonial officials in the following words:

> You have declared to us that it is your earnest desire to live in the strictest union with us, we cannot but approve these good dispositions. We know that treaties have been made for this purpose by our Fathers and agreed to by many of our Old Men yet living. We are sensible that these treaties are binding not only upon those who signed them but upon our whole people and their posterity.

> Yet it would be well that they are renewed and conformed in our days, that the young men may be witnesses to them and transmit a knowledge of them to their children.[44]

The *conventions on tribal sovereignty* approach ultimately traces its ideological design to the Haudenosaunee (or Iroquois) *Kaswentha*, or Two-Row Wampum, model for intergovernmental relations. As with the Haudenosaunee Great Law of Peace, the *Kaswentha* is premised on a foundation of securing peaceful relations with other nations by installing "in government the idea of accountability to future life and responsibility to the seventh generation to come."[45] Further, it embodies an ethic of noninterference in the internal political processes of other nations. The crucible of sovereignty rests within those spaces of intersocietal contact where the polities come together to listen, to discuss, to debate, and to learn. This is the model that I suggest offers the best potential to redirect the trajectory of tribal–federal relations in the direction that reflects the ethos of legal pluralism.

Conclusion

This book has focused attention on the erosion of inherent tribal sovereign powers caused primarily by the legacy of imperialist federal powers that has served to move the nation away from its formative commitments to a legally plural society. It has argued for the acknowledgement and reaffirmation of a more robust and meaningful form of territorial sovereignty for Indian tribes. In presenting this argument, I identified several potential obstacles that may stand in the way of this fuller expression of tribal sovereign power. First, I called attention to certain *ideological* concerns that may complicate this project, namely, our national commitments to liberal democracy and the unitary state model of sovereignty. We discovered, however, that in neither instance are these obstacles insuperable. In reviewing some of the leading scholarship on legal pluralism and liberal theory, I showed that there is ample space to accommodate the interests of tribal nations while meeting our national commitments to individual freedom, equality, and liberty, the core concerns of liberalism. Second, I called attention to certain *constitutional* concerns that may serve to stymie more robust forms of tribal sovereignty. I showed that by employing a revised and more inclusive structuralist approach to constitutional interpretation, the modern Court could avoid reliance on atavistic conceptions of tribal governance and envision tribes as governmental partners, not adversaries, in the goal of securing individual rights and freedoms for all citizens. Finally, I called attention to certain *institutional* forms of intergovernmental relations that have impeded the capacity of tribal governments to secure their political, cultural, and territorial interests. Following a critical assessment of several alternative forms of intergovernmental relations, I suggest a form of bilateralism that borrows from international law that I call *conventions on tribal sovereignty*. Under this rubric, I suggest that tribes are best positioned to advocate for a more robust and secure form of political, cultural, and territorial protection.

In situating tribal sovereignty within the discourse of legal pluralism, I have sought to chart a pathway toward more respectful tribal–federal political relations that will acknowledge and reaffirm a more robust and meaningful form of territorial sovereignty for Indian tribes. The late Anishinabe legal philosopher Perry Shawana wrote that legal pluralism would only aid our understanding of the interactions among different legal systems if it were conceived and operated on the basis of its fundamental elements. For Shawana, those elements are *coexistence*, *independence*, and *complementariness*. In this light, "true legal pluralism can be said to apply when two or more independent legal systems co-exist, operating side by side and interacting in ways that complement each other."[1] With echoes of the conceptual work of Ivison and Tully, Shawana's conceptual framework of legal pluralism posits that the normative legitimacy of each legal system is accepted. The transferability of diverse normative values, practices, and policies from one legal system to another is regulated through negotiation and neither system has an a priori claim to legitimacy or expectation that its legal order must prevail. Perhaps the most compelling feature of Shawana's pluralist approach is his focus on complementariness among the respective legal systems. For Shawana, "each system is strengthened by the existence of the other through actions that contribute to a wider and deeper understanding of each other. As independent yet interdependent systems interact, they strengthen each other through an inherent respect for and understanding of each way of being and knowing. This approach challenges each legal order to set aside questions of legitimacy vis-à-vis itself, and instead to focus on understanding the underpinnings of the law and normative order expressed in the other."[2]

An implicit element underlying Shawana's conceptual framework of legal pluralism, and indeed, the ideological underpinning for my suggested approach of conventions on tribal sovereignty, is the value of humility. Humility is often (mis)associated with weakness or timidity, qualities that seem grossly out of step with the Western preference for, and even obsession with, competition, power and dominance. On closer examination, however, we find that humility also means the absence of arrogance, a posture of openness, and a spirit of deference. The word itself derives from the Latin "humus" which signifies earth or ground. This calls to mind a distinctive feature of the *Ndee* people or White Mountain Apache language, where the tribe employs the same word—*ni*—to signify the concept of "land" and "mind," a powerful expression of the unity between sacred landscapes and one's state of being or identity and the ethic of living in balance with the natural world. From the Apache perspective, the newcomer settlers who arrived and endeavored quickly to exploit and deplete the natural bounty of the environment before moving on to other areas seemed to lack a land ethic, and were, as a consequence, both "landless" and "mindless."[3] The Ndee concept of *ni* illustrates well the wisdom of Shawana's emphasis on complementarity as a foundational element in our understanding of true legal pluralism.

The value of humility in the context of legal pluralism also has significant implications for the protection of liberty, one of liberal democracy's foundational freedoms. The value of humility in relation to liberty is best illustrated by referencing the words of Learned Hand, a prominent legal jurist who served on the federal bench for over a half-century, from 1909 until his death in 1961. For thirty-seven of those years, Judge Hand served on the US Court of Appeal for the Second Circuit. Though he was considered for, but never appointed to the highest court, Judge Hand was widely regarded—then and by many now—as one of America's greatest jurists.

But on May 21, 1944, Judge Hand was not well known outside the legal community, that is, before he gave his famous "Spirit of Liberty" speech in New York's Central Park in front of over 1 million people. The crowd included 150,000 newly naturalized citizens who that day pledged allegiance to their new nation. The nation, of course, was at war and D-Day was only two weeks away.

Judge Hand was among the last speakers to address the immense crowd that day and he challenged his audience to ponder the meaning of liberty. For Judge Hand, this concept had something to do with freedom but not the abstracted freedom that resides in the texts of laws and constitutions and forms the business of the courts. That kind of liberty, said Judge Hand, represents false hopes. "Liberty," he said, "lies in the hearts of men and women; when it dies there, no constitution, no law, no court can save it; no constitution, no law, no court can even do much to help it." He knew what liberty was not: "[It was not] the ruthless, the unbridled will ... the freedom to do as one likes. That is the denial of liberty, and leads straight to its overthrow."[4]

Again he asked the question, "What then is the spirit of liberty?" "I cannot define it," said Judge Hand, "I can only tell you my own faith. The spirit of liberty is the spirit which is not too sure that it is right; the spirit of liberty is the spirit which seeks to understand the minds of other men and women; the spirit of liberty is the spirit which weighs their interests alongside its own without bias."[5] He then asked the audience to rise in "the spirit of that America for which our young men are at this moment fighting and dying" and recite the Pledge of Allegiance.

As Judge Hand's biographer Gerald Gunther notes, this was quite a stunning moment for a federal judge, on a day dripping with nationalist fervor and patriotism, to invoke the spirit of skepticism and humility at a time of war, "a time when," as Gunther says, "unquestioning loyalty to the cause was considered every American's duty."[6] Hand's "Spirit of Liberty" speech would certainly have pleased his mentors from Harvard College, including its president, Charles W. Eliot, from whom Hand would have heard similar exhortations. Eliot's philosophy of education envisioned producing graduates with "an open mind, trained to careful thinking, instructed in the methods of philosophic investigation, acquainted [with] the accumulated thought of past generations, and penetrated with humility."

Within days of Hand's college graduation in June 1893, the *New York Times* ran an editorial that exhibited many of the same qualities of openness and humility. The editorial was a belated acknowledgment, indeed almost a celebration, of the Iroquois and their long-standing confederation of nations, the earliest and most enduring exemplar of legal pluralism in North America. "When that League was formed," said the *Times*, "the white man had not made acquaintance of the Iroquois, if, indeed, Columbus had yet made acquaintance of the American continent. Solely by the Indians themselves was the structure of the League originated. Under the strength of its organization their wonderful work of conquest was carried on.... It was in fact the League itself which gave them their greatest power over all other tribes. In that union there was a degree of strength which no other Indian organization could hope to equal."[7]

The *Times* editorial offered gentle criticism of a recently republished study of federalism by Edward Augustus Freeman for its singular focus on Euro-American contributions to federalist forms of government, effectively ignoring the success of the Iroquois (or Haudenosaunee) in establishing their own enduring forms of confederation. According to the *Times* editors:

> Prof. Freeman takes away from the Americans who created the federal system of the United States none of the glory that belongs to them as originators. They were not conscious imitators of the founders of the Achaian League and they shine not with borrowed light. But the red men also worked without a model. They were the authors of their own powerful institutions. When Prof. Freeman remarks that 'the lawgivers of Achaia and the lawgivers of America are entitled to equal honor,' the praise belongs not alone to Washington and his associates, for, like them, the lawgivers of the Iroquois, out of their own minds and experience, created that formidable political union by which an imperial domain became subject to the Indians of New York."[8]

Enhancing and securing the sovereignty of Indian tribes and redirecting the trajectory of Indian–federal relations in the direction that best reflects the ethos of legal pluralism will inevitably require that we embrace Hand's spirit of liberty. The course of Indian–federal relations will only improve if our approach is marked with openness, humility, and with the spirit that it is not too sure that it is right.

Notes

Front Matter

1. Thomas Cathcart and Daniel Klein, *Plato and a Platypus Walk into a Bar: Understanding Philosophy through Jokes* (New York: Abrams Image, 2007), 17.

Introduction

1. M. B. Hooker, *Legal Pluralism: An Introduction to Colonial and Neo-Colonial Laws* (New York: Oxford University Press, 1975), 1–2.
2. P. G. McHugh, *Aboriginal Societies and the Common Law: A History of Sovereignty, Status, and Self-Determination* (New York: Oxford University Press, 2004), 65.
3. Duncan Ivison, *Postcolonial Liberalism* (Cambridge: University of Cambridge Press, 2002), 154.

Chapter 1

1. *Oliphant v. Suquamish Indian Tribe*, 435 U.S. 191 (1978).
2. For an updated government study of criminal justice issues in Indian country, see United States Government Accountability Office Report (GAO) 11–252 (February 2011), *Indian Country Criminal Justice: Departments of the Interior and Justice Should Strengthen Coordination to Support Tribal Courts*, available at: http://www.gao.gov. See

also Duane Champagne and Carole Goldberg, *Captured Justice: Native Nations and Public Law 280* (Durham, NC: Carolina Academic Press 2012), for a critical review of the effectiveness of state criminal law enforcement in Indian country.

3. *Montana v. United States*, 450 U.S. 544 (1981); *Strate v. A-1 Contractors*, 520 U.S. 438 (1997); *Atkinson Trading Company v. Shirley*, 532 U.S. 645 (2001).
4. *Duro v. Reina,* 495 U.S. 676 (1990).
5. 25 U.S.C. 1301(2).
6. H. Thompson, Minnesota, Op-Ed Comments, *New York Times,* Op-Ed Comments, August 11, 2008.
7. See generally, Roberta Ulrich, *American Indian Nations: From Termination to Restoration, 1953–2006* (Lincoln: University of Nebraska Press, 2010).
8. John Griffiths, "What is Legal Pluralism?" *Journal of Legal Pluralism* 24 (1986): 3.
9. M. B. Hooker, *Legal Pluralism: An Introduction to Colonial and Neo-Colonial Laws* (Oxford: Clarendon Press, 1975), 1.
10. Ibid., 2.
11. Stephen Tierney, *Constitutional Law and National Pluralism* (New York: Oxford University Press, 2004), 4–5.
12. Ibid., 5.
13. Roderick A. MacDonald, "Metaphors of Multiplicity: Civil Society, Regimes and Legal Pluralism," *Arizona Journal of International and Comparative Law* 15 (1998): 74–75.
14. Paul Schiff Berman, "Global Legal Pluralism," *Southern California Law Review* 80 (2007): 1157.
15. Sally Engle Merry, "Legal Pluralism," *Law & Society Review* 22 (1988): 872.
16. Ibid., 874.
17. See, e.g., Brian Z. Tamanaha, "Understanding Legal Pluralism: Past to Present, Local to Global," *Sydney Law Review* 30 (2008): 375.
18. Franz von Benda-Beckmann and Keebet von Benda-Beckmann, "The Dynamics of Change and Continuity in Plural Legal Orders," *Journal of Legal Pluralism*, Vol. 53–54, *Special Double Issue: Dynamics of Plural Legal Orders* (2006): 18.
19. *Cherokee Nation v. Georgia*, 30 U.S. 1, 16 (1831).

20. Ibid., 17.
21. G. Edward White, *The Marshall Court & Cultural Change, 1815–1835*, abridged ed. (New York: Oxford University Press, 1988), 730.
22. *Cherokee Nation v. Georgia,* 30 U.S. 52–53.
23. *Worcester v. Georgia,* 31 U.S. 515, 555 (1832).
24. Ibid., 557.
25. *Notes of Debates in the Federal Convention of 1787, Reported by James Madison* (New York: W.W. Norton & Co., 1987), 477.
26. Ibid., 574.
27. Robert N. Clinton, "The Dormant Indian Commerce Clause," *Connecticut Law Review* 27 (1995): 1164.
28. Act of May 28, 1830, ch. 148, 4 Stat. 411.
29. Robert N. Clinton, "There is No Federal Supremacy Clause for Indian Tribes," *Arizona State Law Journal* 34 (2002): 137, citing VI Gale & Seaton's Register of Debates in Congress, 21st Cong., 1st Sess., Part 2 1059 (May 19, 1830) (emphasis added).
30. *Talton v. Mayes,* 163 U.S. 376, 382 (1896).
31. Francis Paul Prucha, *The Great Father: The United States Government and the American Indians*, abridged ed. (Lincoln: University of Nebraska Press, 1984), 20.
32. Taiaiake Alfred, *Peace, Power and Righteousness: An Indigenous Manifesto* (Ontario: Oxford University Press, 1999), 52.
33. My use of the phrase "formative ethos of legal pluralism" borrows from William E. Connolly's work, most notably his book *The Ethos of Pluralization* (Minneapolis: University of Minnesota Press, 1995). Connolly's work on pluralism is discussed in more detail in chapter 2.
34. See generally Colin G. Calloway, *First Peoples: A Documentary Survey of American Indian History*, 3d ed. (Boston: Bedford/St. Martin's, 2008); Frederick E. Hoxie, *A Final Promise: The Campaign to Assimilate the Indians, 1880–1920* (Cambridge: Cambridge University Press, 1989); Prucha, *The Great Father*; Russell Thornton, *American Indian Holocaust and Survival: A Population History Since 1492* (Norman: University of Oklahoma Press, 1987).
35. *Cohen's Handbook of Federal Indian Law*, ed. Nell Jessup Newton et al. (Newark, NJ: LexisNexis Matthew Bender, 2005), 78.
36. 16 Stat. 566, codified at 25 U.S.C. 71.
37. Kevin Bruyneel, *The Third Space of Sovereignty: The Postcolonial Politics of U.S.–Indigenous Relations* (Minneapolis: University of Minnesota Press, 2007), 70.

38. See, e.g., Russell Lawrence Barsh and James Youngblood Henderson, *The Road: Indian Tribes and Political Liberty* (Berkeley and Los Angeles: University of California Press, 1980), 68–69; Frank Pommersheim, *Broken Landscape: Indians, Indian Tribes, and the Constitution* (New York: Oxford University Press, 2009), 65 ("Little remarked anywhere is the fact that the statute is probably unconstitutional"); Phillip M. Kannan, "Reinstating Treaty-Making with Native American Tribes," *William and Mary Bill of Rights Journal* 16 (2008): 833 ("Section 71 has both of these constitutional fallacies. First, it changes the allocation of authority specified in the Constitution. It does this by denying the President and the Senate, acting together, the authority to enter into treaties with Indian tribes. This change in allocation of power is in conflict with that made by the Constitution. Second, section 71 changes the check and balance dynamics regarding treaty-making with Indian tribes specified in the Constitution"); Comment, "Toward Consent and Cooperation: Reconsidering the Political Status of Indian Nations," *Harvard Civil Rights, Civil Liberties Law Review* 22 (1987): 526 n. 91 ("The 1871 Act arguably violated the separation of powers doctrine, for it eliminated a constitutionally enumerated power of the Executive by legislative act, rather than by constitutional amendment").
39. *United States v. Lara*, 541 U.S. 193, 218 (2004).
40. United Nations Declaration on the Rights of Indigenous Peoples, Article 3, available at: http://www.un.org/esa/socdev/unpfii/en/drip.html.
41. Ibid., Articles 10 and 19.
42. Announcement of U.S. Support for the United Nations Declaration on the Rights of Indigenous Peoples: Initiatives to Promote the Government-to-Government Relationship & Improve the Lives of Indigenous Peoples (Dec. 16, 2010), at 3, available at: http://usun.state.gov/documents/organization/153239.pdf.
43. See *Johnson v. McIntosh*, 21 U.S. 543 (1823) and *Tee-Hit-Ton v. United States*, 348 U.S. 272 (1955); see generally Robert J. Miller, *Native America, Discovered and Conquered: Thomas Jefferson, Lewis and Clark, and Manifest Destiny* (Westport, CT and London: Praeger Publishers, 2006); Steven T. Newcomb, *Pagans in the Promised Land: Decoding the Doctrine of Christian Discovery* (Golden, CO: Fulcrum Publishing, 2008); Lindsay G. Robertson, *Conquest by Law: How the Discovery of America Dispossessed Indigenous Peoples of Their Lands* (New York: Oxford University Press, 2005).

44. Announcement of U.S. Support for the United Nations Declaration on the Rights of Indigenous Peoples, at 5. See also Elvira Pulitano, "Indigenous Rights and International Law: An Introduction," in *Indigenous Rights in the Age of the UN Declaration,* ed. Elvira Pulitano (Cambridge: Cambridge University Press 2012), 7–8.

Chapter 2

1. Renee L. Bergland, *The National Uncanny: Indian Ghosts and American Subjects* (Hanover, NH: Dartmouth College, University Press of New England, 2000), 40.
2. Ibid., 41.
3. Ibid., 40.
4. Ibid., 41, citing Benedict Anderson, *Imagined Communities: Reflection on the Origin and Spread of Nationalism* (New York: Verso, 1991), 6.
5. William E. Connolly, *Pluralism* (Durham, NC: Duke University Press, 2005), 7–8.
6. Ibid., 6–7.
7. Ibid., 7.
8. Ibid., 9.
9. William E. Connolly, *The Ethos of Pluralization* (Minneapolis: University of Minnesota Press, 1995), 180.
10. Ibid., 184.
11. Ibid., 197.
12. Ibid., 163.
13. Ibid., 166.
14. Connolly, *Pluralism*, 142.
15. Connolly, *The Ethos of Pluralization*, 170.
16. Lance Banning, *The Sacred Fire of Liberty: James Madison & the Founding of the Federal Republic* (Ithaca, NY: Cornell University Press, 1995), 131.
17. Ibid., 131.
18. Jeffrey R. Dudas, *The Cultivation of Resentment: Treaty Rights and the New Right* (Stanford, CA: Stanford University Press, 2008), xii.
19. Ibid., 93.
20. *McClanahan v. Arizona State Tax Commission,* 411 U.S. 164 (1973).
21. Ibid., 172.
22. Ibid.

23. Ibid.
24. Plato, *The Republic*, "Book VII: The Cave," translated and with an Introduction by R. E. Allen (New Haven, CT: Yale University Press, 2006), 227–35.
25. *McClanahan v. Arizona State Tax Commission*, 411 U.S. 164, at 173, quoting in part from *United States v. Kagama*, 118 U.S. 375 (1886).
26. *McClanahan v. Arizona State Tax Commission*, 411 U.S. 164, 174-75 (1973).
27. *Talton v. Mayes*, 163 U.S. 376 (1896).
28. *Oliphant v. Suquamish Indian Tribe*, 435 U.S. 191 (1978).
29. The clerk is likely Vicki C. Jackson, newly appointed to the Harvard Law School faculty as the school's first Thurgood Marshall Professor of Constitutional Law. See generally, http://www.law.harvard.edu/news/2011/06/13_vicki-c-jackson.html (last visited on August 6, 2011). See also Todd C. Peppers, *Courtiers of the Marble Palace: The Rise and Influence of the Supreme Court Law Clerk* (Stanford, CA: Stanford University Press, 2006), 226.
30. Bench Memorandum in *Oliphant v. Suquamish Indian Tribe* (undated), Papers of Thurgood Marshall, Collections of the Manuscript Division, Library of Congress (on file with author).
31. *Oliphant v. Suquamish Indian Tribe*, 435 U.S. 191, 208 (1978).
32. *Montana v. United States*, 450 U.S. 544 (1981).
33. Ibid., 559-560 n. 9.
34. Connolly, *The Ethos of Pluralization*, 171.
35. *Confederated Salish & Kootenai Tribes of the Flathead Reservation v. Namen*, 665 F.2d 951, 963-964 n. 30 (1982), *cert. denied*, 459 U.S. 977 (1982).
36. Connolly, *The Ethos of Pluralization*, 180.

Chapter 3

1. Will Kymlicka, *Liberalism, Community and Culture* (New York: Oxford University Press, 1989), 9.
2. See Dale Turner, *This is Not a Peace Pipe: Towards a Critical Indigenous Philosophy* (Toronto: University of Toronto Press, 2006), 13.
3. Kymlicka, *Liberalism, Community and Culture*, 154.
4. See Frank Pommersheim, *Braid of Feathers: American Indian Law and Contemporary Tribal Life* (Berkeley: University of California Press, 1995), 101.

5. Will Kymlicka, *Multicultural Citizenship* (New York: Oxford University Press, 1995), 94.
6. See, e.g., *Boy Scouts of America, et al. v. Dale*, 530 U.S. 640 (2000). See also Angela R. Riley, "(Tribal) Sovereignty and Illiberalism," *California Law Review* 95 (2007): 799.
7. Charles F. Wilkinson, *American Indians, Time, and the Law: Native Societies in a Modern Constitutional Democracy* (New Haven, CT: Yale University Press, 1987), 14.
8. David Schlosberg, "The Pluralist Imagination," in *The Oxford Handbook of Political Theory*, ed. John S. Dryzek, Bonnie Honig and Anne Phillips (New York: Oxford University Press, 2006), 153.
9. Ibid.
10. Ibid., 157.
11. Ibid., 155.
12. Kymlicka, *Liberalism, Community and Culture*, 154.
13. Concurring Opinion of Associate Justice Clarence Thomas in *United States v. Lara,* 541 U.S. 193, 226 (2004).
14. Margaret Moore, "An Historical Argument for Indigenous Self-Determination," in *Secession and Self-Determination*, ed. Stephen Macedo and Allen Buchanan (New York: New York University Press, 2003), 98, citing the work of Jeremy Waldron, "Superseding Historic Injustice," *Ethics* 103 (October 1992): 4–28.
15. Moore, "An Historical Argument for Indigenous Self-Determination," 101.
16. Ibid., 106.
17. John Borrows, *Canada's Indigenous Constitution* (Toronto: University of Toronto Press, 2010), 197, citing the Canadian Supreme Court's decision in *R. v. Van der Peet,* [1996] 2 S.C.R. 507 at 286.
18. Borrows, *Canada's Indigenous Constitution*, 199.
19. Moore, "An Historical Argument for Indigenous Self-Determination," 106–7.
20. Friedrich Kratochwil, "Sovereignty as *Dominium*: Is There a Right of Humanitarian Intervention?" in *Beyond Westphalia? State Sovereignty and International Intervention*, ed. Gene M. Lyons and Michael Mastanduno (Baltimore: Johns Hopkins University Press, 1995), 25.
21. Moore, "An Historical Argument for Indigenous Self-Determination," 107.
22. *Duro v. Reina*, 495 U.S. 676, 685 (1990).

23. Taiaiake Alfred, *Peace, Power, Righteousness: An Indigenous Manifesto* (New York: Oxford University Press, 1999), 48.
24. See 25 U.S.C. 1301, et seq.
25. *Oliphant v. Suquamish Indian Tribe*, 435 U.S. 191, 210 (1978).
26. See generally Wilkinson, *American Indians, Time, and the Law*, 118–19.
27. Duncan Ivison, *Postcolonial Liberalism* (Cambridge: Cambridge University Press 2002), 112–13.
28. Ibid., 11.
29. Ibid., 113.
30. Ibid., 133
31. Ibid., 135.
32. Ibid., 143.
33. *Oliphant v. Suquamish Indian Tribe*, 435 U.S. 191, 210 (1978).
34. *Oliphant v. Schlie*, 544 F.2d 1007, 1013 (9th Cir. 1976).
35. Ibid., 1013-14.
36. Ivison, *Postcolonial Liberalism*, 143.
37. Ibid., 22–23.
38. Ibid., 155.
39. Steven Wheatley, "Indigenous Peoples and the Right of Political Autonomy in an Age of Global Legal Pluralism," in *Law and Anthropology, Current Legal Issues,* Vol. 12, ed. Michael Freeman and David Napier (New York: Oxford University Press, 2008), 351–84, 378, citing Brian Tamanaha, *A General Jurisprudence of Law and Society* (New York: Oxford University Press, 2001), 65.
40. Wheatley, "Indigenous Peoples and the Right of Political Autonomy," 351–84, 377.
41. Tim Schouls, *Shifting Boundaries: Aboriginal Identity, Pluralist Theory, and the Politics of Self-Government* (Vancouver: University of British Columbia Press, 2003), 18.
42. Ibid., 28.
43. Ibid., 30.
44. Ibid., 36.
45. Ibid., 141.
46. Ibid., 179–80.
47. Ibid., 130.
48. Martha-Marie Kleinhans and Roderick A. MacDonald, "What is a Critical Legal Pluralism?" *Canadian Journal of Law and Society* 12 (1997): 25, 36.

49. Stephen Tierney, *Constitutional Law and National Pluralism* (New York: Oxford University Press, 2004), 11.
50. *The State of the Native Nations: Conditions under U.S. Policies of Self-Determination*, Harvard Project on American Indian Economic Development (New York: Oxford University Press, 2008), 352.
51. See generally Donald L. Fixico, *The Urban Indian Experience in America* (Albuquerque: University of New Mexico Press, 2000).
52. *Cohen's Handbook of Federal Indian Law*, ed. Nell Jessup Newton et al. (Newark: LexisNexis Matthew Bender, 2005), 1382.
53. Will Kymlicka, *Multicultural Citizenship* (New York: Oxford University Press, 1995), 189. See also Tierney, *Constitutional Law and National Pluralism*, 339 ("[T]he paradox facing the plurinational state is that the more dominant the constitutional position of the host state national society becomes, the more favourable is the climate for the germination of separatism. The state, therefore, in order to maintain its position externally with its present borders intact, must be prepared to cede power internally so that statehood ceases to be a zero sum game between those states which have it and those sub-state national societies that do not").
54. Burke A. Hendrix, *Ownership, Authority, and Self-Determination* (University Park: Pennsylvania State University Press, 2008), 175.
55. Alfred, *Peace, Power, Righteousness*, 53–59.
56. Dale Turner, *This is Not a Peace Pipe: Towards a Critical Indigenous Philosophy* (Toronto: University of Toronto Press, 2006), 110.
57. Pommersheim, *Braid of Feathers*, 97.
58. *Oliphant v. Suquamish Indian Tribe,* 435 U.S. 191, 209 (1978).
59. Allen E. Buchanan, "The Right to Self-Determination: Analytical and Moral Foundations," *Arizona Journal of International and Comparative Law* 8 (1991): 47.
60. Robert Jackson, *Sovereignty* (Cambridge: Polity Press, 2007), xi.

Chapter 4

1. Michael Dorris, "Indians on the Shelf," in *The American Indian and the Problem of History*, ed. Calvin Martin (New York: Oxford University Press, 1987), 102.
2. My use of the term *peculiarization* is derived from Mark Rifkin, "Indigenizing Agamben: Rethinking Sovereignty in Light of the 'Peculiar' Status of Native Peoples," *Cultural Critique* 73 (2009): 89.

3. Gordon S. Wood, *The Idea of America: Reflections on the Birth of the United States* (New York: Penguin Press, 2011), 233–34.
4. Ibid., 237.
5. Ibid., 321.
6. *Oliphant v. Suquamish Indian Tribe*, 435 U.S. 191, 208–209 (1978).
7. Milner S. Ball, "Stories of Origin and Constitutional Possibilities," in *Michigan Law Review* 87 (1989): 2299.
8. *Johnson v. M'Intosh,* 21 U.S. 543 (1823). The discovery doctrine has been applied in other common law nations to achieve results similar to the one in *Johnson v. M'Intosh*, that is, the legal erasure of indigenous ownership in its ancestral lands save a residual right of occupancy. For a detailed account of the doctrine's application in Australia, Canada, New Zealand, and the United States, see Robert J. Miller, Jacinta Ruru, Larissa Behrendt, and Tracey Lindberg, *Discovering Indigenous Lands: The Doctrine of Discovery in the English Colonies* (New York: Oxford University Press, 2010).
9. *Johnson v. M'Intosh*, 21 U.S. 543, 587 (1823).
10. Ibid., 589.
11. Alex Tallchief Skibine, "Redefining the Status of Indian Tribes within 'Our Federalism': Beyond the Dependency Paradigm," *Connecticut Law Review* 38 (2006): 667.
12. *Johnson v. M'Intosh*, 21 U.S. 543, 593 (1823).
13. Commentary, "Federal Trust Responsibility and Conflicts of Interest—Environmental Protection or Natural Resources Development?" *North Dakota Law Review* 71 (1995): 390–91 (comments of Richard Monette and Robert Clinton).
14. *United States v. Rogers,* 45 U.S. 567 (1846).
15. Ibid., 573.
16. Ibid., 572.
17. Ibid.
18. *United States v. Kagama*, 118 U.S. 375 (1886).
19. See Act of Mar. 3, 1885, Section 9, 23 Stat. 362, codified at 18 U.S.C. 1153.
20. David E. Wilkins, *American Indian Sovereignty and the U.S. Supreme Court: The Masking of Justice* (Austin: University of Texas Press, 1997), 70.
21. Ibid., 70–71.
22. Ibid., 71.
23. *United States v. Kagama*, 118 U.S. 375, 379 (1886).
24. Ibid., 381-82.

25. Ibid., 383–84.
26. See Colin G. Calloway, *First Peoples: A Documentary Survey of American Indian History*, 3d ed. (Boston: Bedford/St. Martin's Press, 2008), 305.
27. T. Alexander Aleinikoff includes the following cases among this class: *Downes v. Bidwell*, 182 U.S. 244 (1901); *Dooley v. United States*, 182 U.S. 222 (1901); *De Lima v. Bidwell*, 182 U.S. 1 (1901); *Armstrong v. United States*, 182 U.S. 243 (1901); and *Dooley v. United States*, 183 U.S. 151 (1901). See T. Alexander Aleinikoff, *Semblances of Sovereignty: The Constitution, the State, and American Citizenship* (Cambridge, MA: Harvard University Press, 2002), 205 n. 55.
28. See generally Aleinikoff, *Semblances of Sovereignty*, 21–31; Walter R. Echo-Hawk, *In the Courts of the Conqueror: The 10 Worst Indian Law Cases Ever Decided* (Golden, CO: Fulcrum Publishing, 2010), 177–80.
29. *Downes v. Bidwell*, 182 U.S. 244, 287 (1901).
30. Aleinikoff, *Semblances of Sovereignty*, 27.
31. *Documents of United States Indian Policy*, 2d ed., ed. Francis Paul Prucha (Lincoln: University of Nebraska Press, 1990), 125.
32. Ibid., 163.
33. See generally Donald L. Drakeman, *Church, State, and Original Intent* (Cambridge: Cambridge University Press, 2010), 305–14.
34. Dawes General Allotment Act of 1887, ch. 119, 24 Stat. 388 (codified as amended at 25 U.S.C. 331–358).
35. *Lone Wolf v. Hitchcock*, 187 U.S. 553 (1903).
36. Ibid., 564.
37. Ibid., 566.
38. Ibid., 565.
39. *Cohen's Handbook of Federal Indian Law*, ed. Nell Jessup Newton et al. (Newark: LexisNexis Matthew Bender, 2005), 48.
40. *Lone Wolf v. Hitchcock*, 187 U.S. 553, 566 (1903).
41. *Chae Chan Ping v. United States*, 130 U.S. 581 (1888).
42. Ibid., 595.
43. Ibid., 595–96.
44. Gabriel J. Chin, "Segregation's Last Stronghold: Race Discrimination and the Constitutional Law of Immigration," *University of California Law Review* 46 (1998): 30, quoting 13 Congressional Record 1584, 2031 (1882) (statement of Rep. Deuster).
45. Indian Citizenship Act of 1924, 43 Stat. 253.

46. Kevin Bruyneel, *The Third Space of Sovereignty: The Postcolonial Politics of U.S.–Indigenous Relations* (Minneapolis: University of Minnesota Press, 2007), 101.
47. Wheeler-Howard Act (Indian Reorganization Act), 48 Stat. 984–988 (1934) (codified as amended at 25 U.S.C. 461 et seq.).
48. Solicitor's Opinion, Powers of Indian Tribes, October 25, 1934, Opinions of the Solicitor, 445.
49. Dalia Tsuk Mitchell, *Architect of Justice: Felix S. Cohen and the Founding of American Legal Pluralism* (Ithaca, NY: Cornell University Press, 2007), 112–13.
50. *On the Drafting of Tribal Constitutions: Felix S. Cohen,* ed. David E. Wilkins (Norman: University of Oklahoma Press, 2006).
51. Ibid., 3.
52. *The State of the Native Nations: Conditions under U.S. Policies of Self-Determination,* The Harvard Project on American Indian Economic Development (New York: Oxford University Press, 2008), 125 ("[T]here must be a consonance (match) between the structure of a society's formal institutions of governance and economic development and its underlying norms of political power and authority (culture) for those institutions to function and serve effectively").
53. *On the Drafting of Tribal Constitutions*, 39.
54. Ibid., 55.
55. Ibid., 134.
56. Mitchell, *Architect of Justice*, 58.
57. It is not entirely clear that Cohen envisioned the collective itself to be a holder of rights, distinct from the rights of its constituent members. See, e.g., *Citizens United v. Federal Election Commission*, 558 U.S. __ (2010), 130 S.Ct. 876 (2010), rejecting federal limits on election-related spending by corporations as violative of corporate rights of free speech.
58. Mitchell, *Architect of Justice*, 115.
59. See Dalia Tsuk (Mitchell), "The New Deal Origins of American Legal Pluralism," *Florida State University Law Review* 29 (2001): 238–39.
60. Indian Claims Commission Act, 62 Stat. 683, Section 2, 60 Stat. 1049 (1946).
61. See Dalia Tsuk (Mitchell), "The New Deal Origins of American Legal Pluralism," 249–50.
62. Mitchell, *Architect of Justice*, 7–8.

63. Ibid., 8.
64. See generally Donald L. Fixico, *Termination and Relocation: Federal Indian Policy, 1945–1960* (Albuquerque: University of New Mexico Press, 1986).
65. Donald L. Fixico, *The Urban Indian Experience in America* (Albuquerque: University of New Mexico Press, 2000); see also Nicholas G. Rosenthal, *Reimagining Indian Country: Native American Migration and Identity in Twentieth-Century Los Angeles* (Chapel Hill: University of North Carolina Press 2012).
66. *Williams v. Lee,* 358 U.S. 217 (1959).
67. Ibid., 220.
68. Ibid., 219 n. 4.
69. Ibid., 221-22.
70. Ibid., 223.
71. For a detailed examination of the case, see Bethany R. Berger, "Sheep, Sovereignty, and the Supreme Court: The Story of *Williams v. Lee*," in *Indian Law Stories*, ed. Carole Goldberg, Kevin K. Washburn, and Philip P. Frickey (New York: Thomson Reuters/Foundation Press, 2011), 359–87.
72. *United States v. Wheeler*, 435 U.S. 313 (1978).
73. Ibid., 326.
74. The citation is from *United States v. Mazurie*, 419 U.S. 544, 557 (1975).
75. *Worcester v. Georgia*, 31 U.S. 515, 557 (1832).
76. Alison L. LaCroix, *The Ideological Origins of American Federalism* (Cambridge: Harvard University Press, 2010).
77. Alison L. LaCroix, "Rhetoric and Reality in Early American Legal History: A Reply to Gordon Wood," *University of Chicago Law Review* 78 (2011): 733.
78. Gordon S. Wood, "Federalism from the Bottom Up," Review of *The Ideological Origins of American Federalism*, Alison L. LaCroix (Harvard University Press, 2010), *University of Chicago Law Review* 78 (2011): 705.
79. LaCroix, *Ideological Origins of American Federalism*, 26.
80. Ibid.
81. Ibid.
82. Ibid., 124.
83. Ibid., 50–51.
84. Ibid., 51.

85. *Oliphant v. Suquamish Indian Tribe*, 435 U.S. 191, 209 (1978).
86. N. Bruce Duthu, "Implicit Divestiture of Tribal Powers: Locating Legitimate Sources of Authority in Indian Country," *American Indian Law Review* 19 (1994): 378–81.
87. *Oliphant v. Suquamish Indian Tribe*, 435 U.S. 191, 208 (1978).
88. Wood, "Federalism from the Bottom Up," 729.
89. Ibid., 710–11.
90. LaCroix, *Ideological Origins of American Federalism*, 229 n. 40.
91. H. W. Brands, *The First American: The Life and Times of Benjamin Franklin* (New York: Anchor Books, 2002), 232–33.
92. Donald A. Grinde, Jr. "Iroquois Political Theory and the Roots of American Democracy," in *Exiled in the Land of the Free: Democracy, Indian Nations, and the U.S. Constitution*, ed. Oren R. Lyons and John C. Mohawk (Santa Fe, NM: Clear Light Publishers, 1992), 263.
93. Dale Turner, *This is Not a Peace Pipe: Towards a Critical Indigenous Philosophy* (Toronto: University of Toronto Press, 2006), 67.
94. Ibid., 66.
95. N. Bruce Duthu, *American Indians and the Law* (New York: Viking Group, 2008), 66.
96. Ibid.
97. See 25 U.S.C. 465. Federal regulations distinguish between acquisition of fee lands located within an existing reservation (25 C.F.R. 151.10) and fee lands located outside a reservation (25 C.F.R. 151.11).
98. Turner, *This is Not a Peace Pipe*, 66.
99. Leland de la Durantaye, *Giorgio Agamben: A Critical Introduction* (Stanford, CA: Stanford University Press, 2009), 206.
100. Giorgio Agamben, *Homo Sacer: Sovereign Power and Bare Life*, trans. Daniel Heller-Roazen (Stanford, CA: Stanford University Press, 1998), 10.
101. de la Durantaye, *Giorgio Agamben*, 228.
102. Ibid., 228.
103. Agamben, *Homo Sacer*, 15.
104. Ibid., 28–29.
105. Mark Rifkin, "Indigenizing Agamben: Rethinking Sovereignty in Light of the 'Peculiar' Status of Native Peoples," *Cultural Critique* 73 (2009): 92–93.
106. Agamben, *Homo Sacer*, 79.
107. Ibid., 105.

108. *Talton v. Mayes,* 163 U.S. 376, 384 (1896).
109. *Documents of United States Indian Policy,* 2d ed., ed. Francis Paul Prucha (Lincoln: University of Nebraska Press, 1990), 2. For an excellent presentation of the historical origins of the "Indian as savage," see Robert A. Williams, Jr., *Savage Anxieties: The Invention of Western Civilization* (New York: Palgrave MacMillan 2012); see also Ann E. Tweedy, "Hostile Indian Tribes … Outlaws, Wolves, … Bears … Grizzlies and Things Like That?' How the Second Amendment and Supreme Court Precedent Target Tribal Self-Defense," *University of Pennsylvania Journal of Constitutional Law* 13 (2011): 687.
110. Agamben, *Homo Sacer,* 39.
111. de la Durantaye, *Giorgio Agamben,* 230.
112. Ibid., 230.
113. Agamben, *Homo Sacer,* 45.
114. de la Durantaye, *Giorgio Agamben,* 232.
115. *United States v. Wheeler,* 435 U.S. 313, 323 (1978).
116. Justice Thurgood Marshall, "Memorandum to the Conference," January 16, 1978, in *United States v. Wheeler,* No. 76–1629, Papers of Thurgood Marshall, Library of Congress (on file with author).
117. Robert A. Williams, Jr., *Like a Loaded Weapon: The Rehnquist Court, Indian Rights, and the Legal History of Racism in America* (Minneapolis: University of Minnesota Press, 2005).
118. *Korematsu v. United States,* 323 U.S. 214 (1944).
119. Ibid., 246.
120. *Morton v. Mancari,* 417 U.S. 535, 555 (1974).
121. See *United States v. Antelope,* 430 U.S. 641 (1977).
122. For a detailed analysis of *Morton v. Mancari,* see Carole Goldberg, "What's Race Got to Do With It? The Story of *Morton v. Mancari,*" in *Indian Law Stories,* ed. Carole Goldberg, Kevin K. Washburn, and Philip P. Frickey (New York: Foundation Press, 2011), 389–420.

Chapter 5

1. *Duro v. Reina,* 495 U.S. 676, 694 (1990).
2. S. 1925, 112th Cong. (2011).
3. Report on H.R. 4970, 112th Cong., 2d. Sess. (May 15, 2012), 58.
4. See, e.g., Timothy Williams, "For Native American Women, Scourge of Rape, Rare Justice," *New York Times,* May 22, 2012, A1; Jefferson Keel,

VAWA Tribal Provisions are Constitutionally Sound, TheHill.com, May 10, 2012, available at: http://thehill.com/blogs/congress-blog/civil-rights/226743-vawa-tribal-provisions-are-constitutionally-sound; Thomas F. Gede, "*Criminal Jurisdiction of Indian Tribes: Should Non-Indians Be Subject to Tribal Criminal Authority Under VAWA?*" Engage Volume 13, Issue 2, July 2012, August 6, 2012, available at: http://www:fed-soc.org/publications/detail/criminal-jurisdiction-of-Indian-tribes-should-non-Indians-be-subject-to-tribal-criminal-authority.

5. Letter from Kevin Washburn, Dean and Professor of Law, University of New Mexico School of Law, et al. to Senator Patrick Leahy (D-VT) et al., Constitutionality of Tribal Government Provisions in VAWA Reauthorization, April 21, 2012.
6. *United States v. Lara*, 541 U.S. 193 (2004).
7. *Duro v. Reina*, 495 U.S. 676 (1990).
8. See Section of Individual Rights and Responsibilities, Report to the House of Delegates, American Bar Association, August 2012 (on file with author).
9. See Jane M. Smith and Richard M. Thompson II, Congressional Research Service, Tribal Criminal Jurisdiction over Non-Indians in the Violence Against Women Act (VAWA) Reauthorization and the SAVE Native Women Act, April 18, 2012.
10. Senate Report 112–153 (2012).
11. 25 U.S.C. 1302.
12. Tribal Law and Order Act of 2010, Pub.L. 111–211, 124 Stat. 2258 (July 29, 2010).
13. See Smith and Thompson, Congressional Research Service, Tribal Criminal Jurisdiction over Non-Indians in the Violence Against Women Act (VAWA) Reauthorization and the SAVE Native Women Act, 4.
14. See ibid., 7. For an even more detailed analysis of the VAWA legislation and the SAVE Native Women Act that reaches the same conclusion as the Congressional Research Service, see Letter to Congress from the National Association of Criminal Defense Lawyers and the National Association of Federal Defenders, *The Violence Against Women Reauthorization Act of 2012 (S. 1925)*, April 23, 2012 (on file with the author).
15. Donald P. Kommers, John E. Finn, and Gary J. Jacobsohn, *American Constitutional Law: Essays, Cases, and Comparative Notes*, Volume 1, *Governmental Powers and Democracy* (Lanham, MD: Rowman & Littlefield Publishers, 2010), 43.

16. Charles L. Black, Jr., *Structure and Relationship in Constitutional Law* (Woodbridge, CT: Ox Bow Press, 1985), 13. (Originally published, Baton Rouge: Louisiana State University Press, 1969).
17. Laurence H. Tribe, *The Invisible Constitution* (New York: Oxford University Press, 2008).
18. Ibid., 147.
19. Ibid., 25.
20. Ibid., 28.
21. Ibid., 34.
22. *Carrington v. Rash,* 380 U.S. 89 (1965).
23. Black, *Structure and Relationship in Constitutional Law*, 11.
24. Ibid., 21.
25. Ibid., 22.
26. Frank J. Colucci, *Justice Kennedy's Jurisprudence: The Full and Necessary Meaning of Liberty* (Lawrence: University Press of Kansas, 2009), 135.
27. Ibid., 136.
28. Alison L. LaCroix, *The Ideological Origins of American Federalism* (Cambridge, MA: Harvard University Press, 2010), 5.
29. See, e.g., *U.S. Term Limits, Inc. v. Thornton*, 514 U.S. 779, 838 (1997) (Kennedy, J., concurring) ("Federalism was our Nation's own discovery. The Framers split the atom of sovereignty. It was the genius of their idea that our citizens would have two political capacities, one state and one federal, each protected by incursion from the other"); *Alden v. Maine*, 527 U.S. 706, 751 (1999) (Kennedy, J., writing for the majority) ("By 'split[ting] the atom of sovereignty', the Founders established 'two orders of government, each with its own direct relationship, its own privity, its own set of mutual rights and obligations to the people who sustain it and are governed by it'. When the Federal Government asserts authority over a State's most fundamental political processes, it strikes at the heart of the political accountability so essential to our liberty and republican form of government").
30. *Clinton v. New York*, 524 U.S. 417 (1998).
31. Colucci, *Justice Kennedy's Jurisprudence*, 142.
32. Ibid., 169.
33. Letter of Daniel K. Akaka, United States Senator and Chairman, US Senate Committee on Indian Affairs, to Tribal Leaders, August 15, 2011, on file with author.
34. *Oliphant v. Schlie*, 544 F.2d 1007 (9th Cir. 1976). The quoted materials are from Justice Kennedy's dissenting opinion in this case from the

Court of Appeals for the Ninth Circuit, the federal appeals court on which Justice Kennedy sat just prior to his elevation to the US Supreme Court.

35. *Oliphant v. Suquamish Indian Tribe*, 435 U.S. 191 (1978).
36. Sarah Krakoff, "Mark the Plumber v. Tribal Empire, or Non-Indian Anxiety v. Tribal Sovereignty?: The Story of *Oliphant v. Suquamish Indian Tribe*," in *Indian Law Stories*, ed. Carol Goldberg, Kevin K. Washburn, and Philip P. Frickey (New York: Thomson Reuters/ Foundation Press, 2011), 261, citing Cynthia Gorney, "Tribal Powers Challenged," *Washington Post*, February 20, 1978, A1.
37. Krakoff, "Mark the Plumber," 272.
38. *Talton v. Mayes,* 163 U.S. 376 (1896).
39. *Ex Parte Crow Dog*, 109 U.S. 556 (1883).
40. *Duro v. Reina*, 495 U.S. 676 (1990). Parenthetical citations in the text are references to this opinion.
41. *Reid v. Covert*, 354 U.S. 1 (1957).
42. Ibid., 39.
43. Colucci, *Justice Kennedy's Jurisprudence*, 143.
44. Letter of Justice Antonin Scalia to Justice William Brennan (April 4, 1990), Papers of Thurgood Marshall, Library of Congress, Washington, DC (on file with author).
45. See Philip S. Deloria and Nell Jessup Newton, "The Criminal Jurisdiction of Tribal Courts over NonMember Indians," *Federal Bar News and Journal* 38 (1991): 70.
46. 25 U.S.C. 1301(2), as amended by Act of October 28, 1991, 105 Stat. 646.
47. *United States v. Lara,* 541 U.S. 193 (2004). Parenthetical citations within the text that follows are referenced to this opinion.
48. *McClanahan v. Arizona Tax Commission*, 411 U.S. 164, 172 n.7 (1973).
49. *Merrion v. Jicarilla Apache Tribe*, 455 U.S. 130, 155 n. 21 (1982).
50. *Cotton Petroleum Corporation v. New Mexico*, 490 U.S. 163, 192 (1989).
51. *United States v. Lara*, 541 U.S. 193, 201 (2004).
52. Frank Pommersheim, *Broken Landscape: Indians, Indian Tribes, and the Constitution* (New York: Oxford University Press, 2009), 151.
53. *United States v. Lara*, 541 U.S. 193, 212–14 (2004).
54. Colucci, *Justice Kennedy's Jurisprudence*, 139.
55. *Oliphant v. Schlie*, 544 F.2d 1007, 1015 n. 3 (9th Cir. 1976).
56. *Alden v. Maine*, 527 U.S. 706 (1999).
57. Ibid., 749.
58. Ibid., 751.

59. *United States v. Lara,* 541 U.S. 193, 224 (2004).
60. Ibid., 218.
61. Ibid.
62. Ibid., 225.
63. Maureen Konkle, "Indigenous Ownership and the Emergence of U.S. Liberal Imperialism," *American Indian Quarterly* 32/3 (2008): 304.
64. *Alden v. Maine*, 527 U.S. 706, 748 (1999).

Chapter 6

1. Hearings on the Nomination of Judge Stephen Breyer to the US Supreme Court, Senate Committee on the Judiciary: S. Hrg. 103–715, 103d Cong., 2d Sess. (1994) (July 13, 1994).
2. *Santa Clara Pueblo v. Martinez,* 436 U.S. 49 (1978). In *Martinez,* the Court declared that with one exception, the tribal courts were the exclusive forums to resolve such claims. Claims challenging the legality of one's detention under tribal law could be brought in federal court under the ICRA's habeas corpus provisions. 25 U.S.C. 1303 ("The privilege of the writ of habeas corpus shall be available to any person, in a court of the United States, to test the legality of his detention by order of an Indian tribe").
3. Frank Pommersheim, *Braid of Feathers: American Indian Law and Contemporary Tribal Life* (Berkeley: University of California Press, 1995), 2.
4. Duncan Ivison, *Postcolonial Liberalism* (Cambridge: Cambridge University Press 2002), 143.
5. 25 U.S.C. 450 et seq.
6. For a brief overview, see *Cohen's Handbook of Federal Indian Law*, ed. Nell Jessup Newton et al. (Newark, NJ: LexisNexis/Matthew Bender, 2005), 103-13.
7. 25 U.S.C. 2701 et seq.
8. Jeff Corntassel and Richard C. Witmer, *Forced Federalism: Contemporary Challenges to Indigenous Nationhood* (Norman: University of Oklahoma Press, 2008), xv.
9. Pommersheim, *Braid of Feathers*, 156.
10. Richard M. Nixon, "Special Message on Indian Affairs" (July 8, 1970) reprinted in *Documents of United States Indian Policy,* 2d ed., ed. Francis Paul Prucha (Lincoln: University of Nebraska Press, 1990), 256.
11. See Tribal Law and Order Act of 2010, Pub. L. No. 111–211, 124 Stat. 2279.

12. Hearings on the Tribal Law and Order Act of 2009, Senate Committee on Indian Affairs: S. Hrg. on S. 797, 111th Cong., 1st Sess. (2009) (October 29, 2009).
13. Troy A. Eid, "Indian Law & Order Commission Moves Ahead," *Indian Country Today*, April 30, 2011, available at: http://indiancountrytodaymedianetwork.com/ict_sbc/indian-law-order-commission-moves-ahead/.
14. Russell Lawrence Barsh and James Youngblood Henderson, *The Road: Indian Tribes and Political Liberty* (Berkeley: University of California Press, 1980).
15. Ibid., 280.
16. Robert N. Clinton, "There is No Federal Supremacy Clause for Indian Tribes," 34 *Arizona State Law Journal* 34 (2002): 258.
17. Frank Pommersheim, *Broken Landscape: Indians, Indian Tribes, and the Constitution* (New York: Oxford University Press, 2009).
18. Ibid., 307.
19. Ibid.
20. Ibid., 309.
21. Kevin Bruyneel, *The Third Space of Sovereignty: The Postcolonial Politics of U.S.–Indigenous Relations* (Minneapolis: University of Minnesota Press, 2007), 165.
22. See, e.g., T. Alexander Aleinikoff, *Semblances of Sovereignty: The Constitution, the State, and American Citizenship* (Cambridge, MA: Harvard University Press, 2002), 140–41; Clinton, "There is No Federal Supremacy Clause for Indian Tribes," 258; Robert A. Williams, Jr., *Linking Arms Together: American Indian Treaty Visions of Law & Peace, 1600–1800* (New York: Oxford University Press, 1997), 124–25.
23. Clinton, "There is No Federal Supremacy Clause for Indian Tribes," 258.
24. Pommersheim, *Broken Landscape*, 308.
25. See generally Williams, *Linking Arms Together*, 124–25.
26. N. Bruce Duthu, *American Indians and the Law* (New York: Viking/Penguin Group, 2008), 213.
27. James Tully, *Strange Multiplicity: Constitutionalism in an Age of Diversity* (Cambridge: Cambridge University Press 1995), 116.
28. Burke A. Hendrix, *Ownership, Authority, and Self-Determination* (University Park: Pennsylvania State University Press, 2008), 153.
29. See, e.g., Bethany Berger, "Justice and the Outsider: Jurisdiction over Nonmembers in Tribal Legal Systems," *Arizona State Law Journal* 37 (2005): 1047.

30. Pommersheim, *Braid of Feathers*, 3.
31. *Oliphant v. Suquamish Indian Tribe,* 435 U.S. 191, 209 (1978).
32. Ivison, *Postcolonial Liberalism*, 154.
33. See, e.g., the habeas corpus provisions of the Indian Civil Rights Act, 25 U.S.C. 1303 ("The privilege of the writ of habeas corpus shall be available to any person, in a court of the United States, to test the legality of his detention by order of an Indian tribe"); *National Farmers Union Insurance Company v. Crow Tribe*, 471 U.S. 845 (1985) (allowing access to federal court under its *federal question jurisdiction* to challenge tribal jurisdiction after the litigant has exhausted tribal remedies).
34. See, e.g., *Rice v. Cayetano*, 528 U.S. 495 (2000).
35. *Lewis v. Norton*, 424 F.3d 959, 963 (9th Cir. 2005).
36. See generally Circe Sturm, *Blood Politics: Race, Culture, and Identity in the Cherokee Nation of Oklahoma* (Berkeley: University of California Press 2002).
37. See Celia E. Naylor, *African Cherokees in Indian Territory: From Chattel to Citizens* (Chapel Hill: University of North Carolina Press 2008), 201–19; Duthu, *American Indians and the Law*, 156–57.
38. See Brian Klopotek, *Recognition Odysseys: Indigeneity, Race, and Federal Recognition Policy in Three Louisiana Indian Communities* (Durham, NC: Duke University Press 2011), 8.
39. *Santa Clara Pueblo v. Martinez*, 436 U.S. 49, 72 n. 32 (1978).
40. Evelyn Nieves, "Putting to a Vote the Question 'Who is Cherokee?'" *New York Times*, March 3, 2007, available at: http://www.nytimes.com/2007/03/03/us/03cherokee.html.
41. *Snowden v. Saginaw Chippewa Indian Tribe of Michigan*, 32 Indian Law Reporter 6047, 6050 (Saginaw Chippewa Indian Tribe of Michigan Appellate Court 2005).
42. See, e.g., Suzianne D. Painter-Thorne, "If you Build It, They Will Come: Preserving Tribal Sovereignty in the Face of Indian Casinos & the New Premium on Tribal Membership," *Lewis & Clark Law Review* 14 (2010): 311.
43. Williams, *Linking Arms Together*, 112.
44. Ibid.
45. Oren R. Lyons, "The American Indian in the Past," in *Exiled in the Land of the Free: Democracy, Indian Nations, and the U.S. Constitution*, ed. Oren R. Lyons and John C. Mohawk (Santa Fe, NM: Clear Light Publishers, 1992), 33.

Conclusion

1. Perry Shawana, "Legal Processes, Pluralism in Canadian Jurisprudence, and the Governance of the Carrier Medicine Knowledge," in *Indigenous Legal Traditions*, ed. Law Commission of Canada (Vancouver: University of British Columbia Press, 2007), 128.
2. Ibid., 129.
3. See John R. Welch and Ramon Riley, "Reclaiming Land and Spirit in the Western Apache Homeland," *American Indian Quarterly* 25/1 (2001): 5–12.
4. Gerald Gunther, *Learned Hand: The Man and the Judge* (Cambridge, MA: Harvard University Press, 1994), 548–49.
5. Ibid., 549.
6. Ibid., 552.
7. Robert Hays, *Editorializing "The Indian Problem:" The New York Times on Native Americans, 1860–1900* (Carbondale: Southern Illinois University Press, 1997), 346.
8. Ibid., 346–47.

Bibliography

Cases Cited

Alden v. Maine, 527 U.S. 706 (1999).
Atkinson Trading Company v. Shirley, 532 U.S. 645 (2001).
Boy Scouts of America, et al. v. Dale, 530 U.S. 640 (2000).
Carrington v. Rash, 380 U.S. 89 (1965).
Chae Chan Ping v. United States, 130 U.S. 581 (1888).
Cherokee Nation v. Georgia, 30 U.S. 1 (1831).
Clinton v. New York, 524 U.S. 417 (1998).
Confederated Salish & Kootenai Tribes of the Flathead Reservation v. Namen, 665 F.2d 951 (1982), *cert. denied*, 459 U.S. 977 (1982).
Cotton Petroleum Corporation v. New Mexico, 490 U.S. 163 (1989).
Downes v. Bidwell, 182 U.S. 244 (1901).
Duro v. Reina, 495 U.S. 676 (1990).
Ex Parte Crow Dog, 109 U.S. 556 (1883).
Johnson v. McIntosh, 21 U.S. 543 (1823).
Korematsu v. United States, 323 U.S. 214 (1944).
Lewis v. Norton, 424 F.3d 959 (9th Cir. 2005).
Lone Wolf v. Hitchcock, 187 U.S. 553 (1903).
McClanahan v. Arizona State Tax Commission, 411 U.S. 164 (1973).
Merrion v. Jicarilla Apache Tribe, 455 U.S. 130 (1982).
Montana v. United States, 450 U.S. 544 (1981).
Morton v. Mancari, 417 U.S. 535 (1974).
National Farmers Union Insurance Company v. Crow Tribe, 471 U.S. 845 (1985).
Oliphant v. Schlie, 544 F.2d 1007 (9th Cir. 1976).

Oliphant v. Suquamish Indian Tribe, 435 U.S. 191 (1978).
R. v. Van der Peet, [1996] 2 S.C.R. 507.
Reid v. Covert, 354 U.S. 1 (1957).
Rice v. Cayetano, 528 U.S. 495 (2000).
Santa Clara Pueblo v. Martinez, 436 U.S. 49 (1978).
Snowden v. Saginaw Chippewa Indian Tribe of Michigan, 32 Indian Law Reporter 6047 (Saginaw Chippewa Indian Tribe of Michigan Appellate Court 2005).
Strate v. A-1 Contractors, 520 U.S. 438 (1997).
Talton v. Mayes, 163 U.S. 376 (1896).
Tee-Hit-Ton v. United States, 348 U.S. 272 (1955).
United States v. Antelope, 430 U.S. 641 (1977).
United States v. Kagama, 118 U.S. 375 (1886).
United States v. Lara, 541 U.S. 193 (2004).
United States v. Mazurie, 419 U.S. 544 (1975).
United States v. Rogers, 45 U.S. 567 (1846).
United States v. Wheeler, 435 U.S. 313 (1978).
U.S. Term Limits, Inc. v. Thornton, 514 U.S. 779 (1997).
Williams v. Lee, 358 U.S. 217 (1959).
Worcester v. Georgia, 31 U.S. 515 (1832).

Legislation, Government Documents, and Other Primary Sources

Announcement of U.S. Support for the United Nations Declaration on the Rights of Indigenous Peoples: Initiatives to Promote the Government-to-Government Relationship & Improve the Lives of Indigenous Peoples. Dec. 16, 2010, available at: http://usun.state.gov/documents/organization/153239.pdf.
Cohen's Handbook of Federal Indian Law. Edited by Nell Jessup Newton et al. Newark, NJ: LexisNexis Matthew Bender, 2005.
Dawes General Allotment Act of 1887, ch. 119, 24 Stat. 388 (codified as amended at 25 U.S.C. 331–358).
Documents of United States Indian Policy. 2d ed. Edited by Francis Paul Prucha. Lincoln: University of Nebraska Press, 1990.
Hearings on the Nomination of Judge Stephen Breyer to the US Supreme Court, Senate Committee on the Judiciary: S. Hrg. 103–715, 103d Cong., 2d Sess. (1994) (July 13, 1994).

Hearings on the Tribal Law and Order Act of 2009, Senate Committee on Indian Affairs: S. Hrg. on S. 797, 111th Cong., 1st Sess. (2009) (October 29, 2009).

Indian Citizenship Act of 1924, 43 Stat. 253.

Indian Civil Rights Act of 1968, 25 U.S.C. 1303.

Indian Claims Commission Act of 1946, 60 Stat. 1049, (codified at 28 U.S.C. 1505).

Indian Removal Act of 1830, ch. 148, 4 Stat. 411.

Letter of Daniel K. Akaka, United States Senator and Chairman, US Senate Committee on Indian Affairs, to Tribal Leaders, August 15, 2011.

Letter to Congress from the National Association of Criminal Defense Lawyers and the National Association of Federal Defenders, The Violence Against Women Reauthorization Act of 2012 (S. 1925), April 23, 2012.

Nixon, Richard M. "Special Message on Indian Affairs," July 8, 1970. Reprinted in *Documents of United States Indian Policy*, 2d ed., edited by Francis Paul Prucha. Lincoln: University of Nebraska Press, 1990.

Notes of Debates in the Federal Convention of 1787, Reported by James Madison. New York: W. W. Norton & Co., 1987.

Papers of Thurgood Marshall, Collections of the Manuscript Division, Library of Congress (Washington, DC).

Plato. *The Republic*, "Book VII: The Cave." Translated and with an Introduction by R. E. Allen. New Haven, CT: Yale University Press, 2006.

Smith, Jane M., and Richard M. Thompson II. Congressional Research Service, Tribal Criminal Jurisdiction over Non-Indians in the Violence Against Women Act VAWA Reauthorization and the SAVE Native Women Act, April 18, 2012.

Solicitor's Opinion. Powers of Indian Tribes, October 25, 1934. Opinions of the Solicitor, 445.

The State of the Native Nations: Conditions under U.S. Policies of Self-Determination. Harvard Project on American Indian Economic Development. New York: Oxford University Press, 2008.

Tribal Law and Order Act of 2010, Pub.L. 111–211, 124 Stat. 2258 (July 29, 2010).

United Nations Declaration on the Rights of Indigenous Peoples, Article 3, available at: http://www.un.org/esa/socdev/unpfii/en/drip.html.

United States Government Accountability Office Report (GAO) 11–252 (February 2011). *Indian Country Criminal Justice: Departments of the Interior and Justice Should Strengthen Coordination to Support Tribal Courts*, available at: http://www.gao.gov.

Washburn, Kevin, former Dean and Professor of Law, University of New Mexico School of Law, et al. Letter to Senator Patrick Leahy D-VT et al., Constitutionality of Tribal Government Provisions in VAWA Reauthorization, April 21, 2012.

Wheeler-Howard Act (Indian Reorganization Act), 48 Stat. 984–988 (1934) (codified as amended at 25 U.S.C. 461 et seq.).

Secondary Sources

Agamben, Giorgio. *Homo Sacer: Sovereign Power and Bare Life.* Translated by Daniel Heller-Roazen. Stanford, CA: Stanford University Press, 1998.

Aleinikoff, T. Alexander. *Semblances of Sovereignty: The Constitution, the State, and American Citizenship.* Cambridge, MA: Harvard University Press, 2002.

Alfred, Taiaiake. *Peace, Power and Righteousness: An Indigenous Manifesto.* Ontario: Oxford University Press, 1999.

Anderson, Benedict. *Imagined Communities: Reflection on the Origin and Spread of Nationalism.* New York: Verso, 1991.

Ball, Milner S. "Stories of Origin and Constitutional Possibilities." *Michigan Law Review* 87 (1989): 2280–2319.

Banning, Lance. *The Sacred Fire of Liberty: James Madison and the Founding of the Federal Republic.* Ithaca, NY: Cornell University Press, 1995.

Barsh, Russell Lawrence, and James Youngblood Henderson. *The Road: Indian Tribes and Political Liberty.* Berkeley and Los Angeles: University of California Press, 1980.

Berger, Bethany. "Justice and the Outsider: Jurisdiction over Nonmembers in Tribal Legal Systems." *Arizona State Law Journal* 37 (2005): 1047.

———. "Sheep, Sovereignty, and the Supreme Court: The Story of *Williams v. Lee.*" In *Indian Law Stories*, edited by Carole Goldberg, Kevin K. Washburn, and Philip P. Frickey. New York: Thomson Reuters/Foundation Press, 2011.

Bergland, Renee L. *The National Uncanny: Indian Ghosts and American Subjects.* Hanover, NH: Dartmouth College, University Press of New England, 2000.

Berman, Paul Schiff. "Global Legal Pluralism." *Southern California Law Review* 80 (2007): 1155.

Black, Jr., Charles L. *Structure and Relationship in Constitutional Law.* Woodbridge, CT: Ox Bow Press, 1985. Originally published, Baton Rouge: Louisiana State University Press, 1969.

Borrows, John. *Canada's Indigenous Constitution.* Toronto: University of Toronto Press, 2010.

Brands, H.W. *The First American: The Life and Times of Benjamin Franklin.* New York: Anchor Books, 2002.

Bruyneel, Kevin. *The Third Space of Sovereignty: The Postcolonial Politics of U.S.–Indigenous Relations.* Minneapolis: University of Minnesota Press, 2007.

Buchanan, Allen E. "The Right to Self-Determination: Analytical and Moral Foundations." *Arizona Journal of International and Comparative Law* 8 (1991): 41.

Calloway, Colin G. *First Peoples: A Documentary Survey of American Indian History.* 3d ed. Boston: Bedford/St. Martin's, 2008.

Cathcart, Thomas, and Daniel Klein. *Plato and a Platypus Walk into a Bar: Understanding Philosophy through Jokes.* New York: Abrams Image, 2007.

Champagne, Duane, and Carole Goldberg. *Captured Justice: Native Nations and Public Law.* Durham, NC: Carolina Academic Press, 2012.

Chin, Gabriel J. "Segregation's Last Stronghold: Race Discrimination and the Constitutional Law of Immigration." *University of California Law Review* 46 (1998): 1.

Clinton, Robert N. "The Dormant Indian Commerce Clause." *Connecticut Law Review* 27 (1995): 1055.

———. "There is No Federal Supremacy Clause for Indian Tribes." *Arizona State Law Journal* 34 (2002): 113.

Colucci, Frank J. *Justice Kennedy's Jurisprudence: The Full and Necessary Meaning of Liberty.* Lawrence, KS: University Press of Kansas, 2009.

Commentary. "Federal Trust Responsibility and Conflicts of Interest—Environmental Protection or Natural Resources Development?" *North Dakota Law Review* 71 (1995): 273.

Comment. "Toward Consent and Cooperation: Reconsidering the Political Status of Indian Nations." *Harvard Civil Rights, Civil Liberties Law Review* 22 (1987): 507.

Connolly, William E. *The Ethos of Pluralization.* Minneapolis: University of Minnesota Press, 1995.

———. *Pluralism*. Durham, NC: Duke University Press, 2005.

Corntassel, Jeff, and Richard C. Witmer. *Forced Federalism: Contemporary Challenges to Indigenous Nationhood*. Norman, OK: University of Oklahoma Press, 2008.

de la Durantaye, Leland. *Giorgio Agamben: A Critical Introduction*. Stanford, CA: Stanford University Press, 2009.

Deloria, Philip S., and Nell Jessup Newton. "The Criminal Jurisdiction of Tribal Courts Over NonMember Indians." *Federal Bar News and Journal* 38 (1991): 70.

Dorris, Michael. "Indians on the Shelf." In *The American Indian and the Problem of History*, edited by Calvin Martin. New York: Oxford University Press, 1987.

Drakeman, Donald L. *Church, State, and Original Intent*. Cambridge: Cambridge University Press, 2010.

Dudas, Jeffrey R. *The Cultivation of Resentment: Treaty Rights and the New Right*. Stanford, CA: Stanford University Press, 2008.

Duthu, N. Bruce. *American Indians and the Law*. New York: Viking Group, 2008.

———. "Implicit Divestiture of Tribal Powers: Locating Legitimate Sources of Authority in Indian Country." *American Indian Law Review* 19 (1994): 353.

Echo Hawk, Walter R. *In the Courts of the Conqueror: The 10 Worst Indian Law Cases Ever Decided*. Golden, CO: Fulcrum Publishing, 2010.

Eid, Troy A. "Indian Law & Order Commission Moves Ahead." *Indian Country Today* April 30, 2011.

Fixico, Donald L. *Termination and Relocation: Federal Indian Policy, 1945–1960*. Albuquerque: University of New Mexico Press, 1986.

———. *The Urban Indian Experience in America*. Albuquerque: University of New Mexico Press, 2000.

Gede, Thomas F. "Criminal Jurisdiction of Indian Tribes: Should Non-Indians Be Subject to Tribal Criminal Authority Under VAWA?" Engage Volume 13, Issue 2, July 2012, August 6, 2012, available at: http://www:fed-soc.org/publications/detail/criminal-jurisdiction-of- Indian-tribes-should-non-Indians-be-subject-to-tribal-criminal- authority.

Goldberg, Carole. "What's Race Got to Do With It? The Story of *Morton v. Mancari*." In *Indian Law Stories*, edited by Carole Goldberg, Kevin K. Washburn, and Philip P. Frickey. New York: Foundation Press, 2011.

Griffiths, John. "What is Legal Pluralism?" *Journal of Legal Pluralism* 24 (1986): 1.

Grinde, Jr., Donald A. "Iroquois Political Theory and the Roots of American Democracy." In *Exiled in the Land of the Free: Democracy, Indian Nations, and the U.S. Constitution*, edited by Oren R. Lyons and John C. Mohawk. Santa Fe, NM: Clear Light Publishers, 1992.

Gunther, Gerald. *Learned Hand: The Man and the Judge.* Cambridge, MA: Harvard University Press, 1994.

Hays, Robert. *Editorializing "The Indian Problem:" The New York Times on Native Americans, 1860–1900.* Carbondale: Southern Illinois University Press, 1997.

Hendrix, Burke A. *Ownership, Authority, and Self-Determination.* University Park: Pennsylvania State University Press, 2008.

Hooker, M. B. *Legal Pluralism: An Introduction to Colonial and Neo-Colonial Laws.* New York: Oxford University Press, 1975.

Hoxie, Frederick E. *A Final Promise: The Campaign to Assimilate the Indians, 1880–1920.* Cambridge: Cambridge University Press, 1989.

Ivison, Duncan. *Postcolonial Liberalism.* Cambridge: University of Cambridge Press, 2002.

Jackson, Robert. *Sovereignty.* Cambridge: Polity Press, 2007.

Kannan, Phillip M. "Reinstating Treaty-Making with Native American Tribes." *William and Mary Bill of Rights Journal* 16 (2008): 809.

Keel, Jefferson. *VAWA Tribal Provisions are Constitutionally Sound*, TheHill.com, May 10, 2012, available at: http://thehill.com/blogs/congress-blog/civil-rights/226743-vawa-tribal-provisions-are-constitutionally-sound.

Kleinhans, Martha-Marie, and Roderick A. MacDonald. "What is a Critical Legal Pluralism?" *Canadian Journal of Law and Society* 12 (1997): 25.

Klopotek, Brian. *Recognition Odysseys: Indigeneity, Race, and Federal Recognition Policy in Three Louisiana Indian Communities.* Durham, NC: Duke University Press, 2011.

Kommers, Donald P., John E. Finn, and Gary J. Jacobsohn. *American Constitutional Law: Essays, Cases, and Comparative Notes*, Volume 1, *Governmental Powers and Democracy.* Lanham, MD: Rowman & Littlefield Publishers, 2010.

Konkle, Maureen. "Indigenous Ownership and the Emergence of U.S. Liberal Imperialism." *American Indian Quarterly* 32/3 (2008): 297.

Krakoff, Sarah. "Mark the Plumber v. Tribal Empire, or Non-Indian Anxiety v. Tribal Sovereignty?: The Story of *Oliphant v. Suquamish Indian Tribe*." In *Indian Law Stories*, edited by Carol Goldberg, Kevin K. Washburn, and Philip P. Frickey. New York: Thomson Reuters/ Foundation Press, 2011.

Kratochwil, Friedrich. "Sovereignty as *Dominium*: Is There a Right of Humanitarian Intervention?" In *Beyond Westphalia? State Sovereignty and International Intervention*, edited by Gene M. Lyons and Michael Mastanduno. Baltimore: Johns Hopkins University Press, 1995.

Kymlicka, Will. *Liberalism, Community and Culture*. New York: Oxford University Press, 1989.

———. *Multicultural Citizenship*. New York: Oxford University Press, 1995.

LaCroix, Alison L. *The Ideological Origins of American Federalism*. Cambridge, MA: Harvard University Press, 2010.

———. "Rhetoric and Reality in Early American Legal History: A Reply to Gordon Wood." *University of Chicago Law Review* 78 (2011): 733.

Lyons, Oren R. "The American Indian in the Past." In *Exiled in the Land of the Free: Democracy, Indian Nations, and the U.S. Constitution*, edited by Oren R. Lyons and John C. Mohawk. Santa Fe, NM: Clear Light Publishers, 1992.

MacDonald, Roderick A. "Metaphors of Multiplicity: Civil Society, Regimes and Legal Pluralism." *Arizona Journal of International and Comparative Law* 15 (1998): 69.

McHugh, P. G. *Aboriginal Societies and the Common Law: A History of Sovereignty, Status, and Self-Determination*. New York: Oxford University Press, 2004.

Merry, Sally Engle. "Legal Pluralism." *Law & Society Review* 22 (1988): 869.

Miller, Robert J. *Native America, Discovered and Conquered: Thomas Jefferson, Lewis and Clark, and Manifest Destiny*. Westport, CT and London: Praeger Publishers, 2006.

Miller, Robert J., Jacinta Ruru, Larissa Behrendt, and Tracey Lindberg. *Discovering Indigenous Lands: The Doctrine of Discovery in the English Colonies*. New York: Oxford University Press, 2010.

Mitchell, Dalia Tsuk. *Architect of Justice: Felix S. Cohen and the Founding of American Legal Pluralism*. Ithaca, NY: Cornell University Press, 2007.

———. "The New Deal Origins of American Legal Pluralism." *Florida State University Law Review* 29 (2001): 189.

Moore, Margaret. "An Historical Argument for Indigenous Self-Determination." In *Secession and Self-Determination*, edited by Stephen Macedo and Allen Buchanan. New York: New York University Press, 2003.

Naylor, Celia E. *African Cherokees in Indian Territory: From Chattel to Citizens.* Chapel Hill, NC: University of North Carolina Press, 2008.

Newcomb, Steven T. *Pagans in the Promised Land: Decoding the Doctrine of Christian Discovery*. Golden, CO: Fulcrum Publishing, 2008.

Nieves, Evelyn. "Putting to a Vote the Question 'Who is Cherokee?'" *New York Times*, March 3, 2007.

Painter-Thorne, Suzianne D. "If you Build It, They Will Come: Preserving Tribal Sovereignty in the Face of Indian Casinos & the New Premium on Tribal Membership." *Lewis & Clark Law Review* 14 (2010): 311.

Peppers, Todd C. *Courtiers of the Marble Palace: The Rise and Influence of the Supreme Court Law Clerk*. Stanford, CA: Stanford University Press, 2006.

Pommersheim, Frank. *Braid of Feathers: American Indian Law and Contemporary Tribal Life.* Berkeley: University of California Press, 1995.

———. *Broken Landscape: Indians, Indian Tribes, and the Constitution.* New York: Oxford University Press, 2009.

Prucha, Francis Paul. *The Great Father: The United States Government and the American Indians.* Abridged edition. Lincoln: University of Nebraska Press, 1984.

Pulitano, Elvira. "Indigenous Rights and International Law: An Introduction." In *Indigenous Rights in the Age of the UN Declaration,* edited by Elvira Pulitano. Cambridge: Cambridge University Press, 2012.

Rifkin, Mark. "Indigenizing Agamben: Rethinking Sovereignty in Light of the 'Peculiar' Status of Native Peoples." *Cultural Critique* 73 (2009): 89.

Riley, Angela R. "Tribal Sovereignty and Illiberalism." *California Law Review* 95 (2007): 799.

Robertson, Lindsay G. *Conquest by Law: How the Discovery of America Dispossessed Indigenous Peoples of Their Lands.* New York: Oxford University Press, 2005.

Rosenthal, Nicolas G. *Reimagining Indian Country: Native American Migration & Identity in Twentieth-Century Los Angeles*. Chapel Hill: University of North Carolina Press, 2012.

Schlosberg, David. "The Pluralist Imagination." In *The Oxford Handbook of Political Theory*, edited by John S. Dryzek, Bonnie Honig, and Anne Phillips. New York: Oxford University Press, 2006.

Schouls, Tim. *Shifting Boundaries: Aboriginal Identity, Pluralist Theory, and the Politics of Self-Government.* Vancouver: University of British Columbia Press, 2003.

Shawana, Perry. "Legal Processes, Pluralism in Canadian Jurisprudence, and the Governance of the Carrier Medicine Knowledge." In *Indigenous Legal Traditions*, edited by Law Commission of Canada. Vancouver: University of British Columbia Press, 2007.

Skibine, Alex Tallchief. "Redefining the Status of Indian Tribes within 'Our Federalism': Beyond the Dependency Paradigm." *Connecticut Law Review* 38 (2006): 667.

Sturm, Circe. *Blood Politics: Race, Culture, and Identity in the Cherokee Nation of Oklahoma.* Berkeley: University of California Press, 2002.

Tamanaha, Brian. *A General Jurisprudence of Law and Society.* New York: Oxford University Press, 2001.

———. "Understanding Legal Pluralism: Past to Present, Local to Global." *Sydney Law Review* 30 (2008): 375.

Thompson, H. Op-Ed Comments. *New York Times,* August 11, 2008.

Thornton, Russell. *American Indian Holocaust and Survival: A Population History since 1492.* Norman: University of Oklahoma Press, 1987.

Tierney, Stephen. *Constitutional Law and National Pluralism.* New York: Oxford University Press, 2004.

Tribe, Laurence H. *The Invisible Constitution.* New York: Oxford University Press, 2008.

Tully, James. *Strange Multiplicity: Constitutionalism in an Age of Diversity.* Cambridge: Cambridge University Press, 1995.

Turner, Dale. *This is Not a Peace Pipe: Towards a Critical Indigenous Philosophy.* Toronto: University of Toronto Press, 2006.

Tweedy, Ann E. "Hostile Indian Tribes … Outlaws, Wolves, … Bears … Grizzlies and Things Like That?' How the Second Amendment and Supreme Court Precedent Target Tribal Self-Defense." *University of Pennsylvania Journal of Constitutional Law* 13 (2011): 687.

Ulrich, Roberta. *American Indian Nations from Termination to Restoration, 1953–2006.* Lincoln: University of Nebraska Press, 2010.

Von Benda-Beckmann, Franz, and Keebet Von Benda-Beckmann. "The Dynamics of Change and Continuity in Plural Legal Orders."

Journal of Legal Pluralism, Vol. 53–54, *Special Double Issue: Dynamics of Plural Legal Orders* 2006.

Waldron, Jeremy. "Superseding Historic Injustice." *Ethics* (October 1992): 103.

Welch, John R., and Ramon Riley. "Reclaiming Land and Spirit in the Western Apache Homeland." *American Indian Quarterly* 25/1 (2001): 5.

Wheatley, Steven. "Indigenous Peoples and the Right of Political Autonomy in an Age of Global Legal Pluralism." In *Law and Anthropology, Current Legal Issues, Volume 12*, edited by Michael Freeman and David Napier. New York: Oxford University Press, 2008.

White, G. Edward. *The Marshall Court and Cultural Change, 1815–1835*. Abridged edition. New York: Oxford University Press, 1988.

Wilkins, David E. *American Indian Sovereignty and the U.S. Supreme Court: The Masking of Justice*. Austin: University of Texas Press, 1997.

———. Ed. *On the Drafting of Tribal Constitutions: Felix S. Cohen*. Norman: University of Oklahoma Press, 2006.

Wilkinson, Charles F., *American Indians, Time, and the Law: Native Societies in a Modern Constitutional Democracy*. New Haven, CT: Yale University Press, 1987.

Williams, Jr., Robert A. *Like a Loaded Weapon: The Rehnquist Court, Indian Rights, and the Legal History of Racism in America*. Minneapolis: University of Minnesota Press, 2005.

———. *Linking Arms Together: American Indian Treaty Visions of Law and Peace, 1600–1800*. New York: Oxford University Press, 1997.

———. *Savage Anxieties: The Invention of Western Civilization*. New York: Palgrave MacMillan, 2012.

Williams, Timothy. "For Native American Women, Scourge of Rape, Rare Justice." *New York Times*, May 22, 2012, A1.

Wood, Gordon S. "Federalism from the Bottom Up." Review of *The Ideological Origins of American Federalism*, Alison L. LaCroix, Harvard University Press, 2010. *University of Chicago Law Review* 78 (2011): 705.

———. *The Idea of America: Reflections on the Birth of the United States*. New York: Penguin Press, 2011.

Index